First World War
and Army of Occupation
War Diary
France, Belgium and Germany

1 INDIAN CAVALRY DIVISION
Headquarters, Branches and Services
Royal Army Veterinary Corps
Assistant Director Veterinary Services
1 July 1916 - 31 December 1916

WO95/1169/3

The Naval & Military Press Ltd
www.nmarchive.com
Published in association with The National Archives

Published by

The Naval & Military Press Ltd

Unit 10 Ridgewood Industrial Park,

Uckfield, East Sussex,

TN22 5QE England

Tel: +44 (0) 1825 749494

www.naval-military-press.com

www.nmarchive.com

This diary has been reprinted in facsimile from the original. Any imperfections are inevitably reproduced and the quality may fall short of modern type and cartographic standards.

© **Crown Copyright**
Images reproduced by permission of The National Archives, London, England, 2015.

Contents

Document type	Place/Title	Date From	Date To
Heading	WO95/1169/3		
Heading	1 Ind Cav Div A D V S 1916 July 1916 Dec		
Heading	War Diary of A D V S 1st Indian Cavalry Division From 1st July 1916 To 31st July 1916		
War Diary	War Diary of Assistant Director Of Veterinary Services 1st Indian Cavalry Division From 1st July 1916 To 31st July 1916		
War Diary	Doullens	01/07/1916	01/07/1916
War Diary	Auxi-Le-Chateau	02/07/1916	18/07/1916
War Diary	Savy-Berlette	19/07/1916	31/07/1916
Heading	War Diary of A D V S 1st Indian Cavalry Division From 1st August 1916 To 31 August 1916		
War Diary	Savy-Berlette	01/08/1916	31/08/1916
Heading	War Diary of A D V S 1st Indian Cavalry Division From 1st September 1916 To 31st September 1916		
War Diary	S Riquier	04/09/1916	13/09/1916
War Diary	Allonville	15/09/1916	30/09/1916
Heading	War Diary of A D V S 4th Cavalry Division (late 1st Ind Cavy Divn) From 1st October 1916 To 30th November 1916		
War Diary	Ligescourt	01/10/1916	01/10/1916
War Diary	Wadicourt	02/10/1916	31/10/1916
War Diary	War Diary of Assistant Director Of Veterinary Service 4th Cavalry Division. From 1-11-16 To 30-11-16 Volume V		
War Diary	Bernay	01/11/1916	01/11/1916
War Diary	St Valery	02/11/1916	30/11/1916
Heading	War Diary of A D V S 4th Cavalry Division From 1st December 1916 To 31st December 1916		
War Diary	St. Valery	01/12/1916	31/12/1916

WO 95/1169/3

| IND CAN JAP | AUS | 1916 JUN — 1916 DEC |

SERIAL NO 322

Confidential War Diary

of

A.D.V.S., 1st Indian Cavalry Division.

FROM 1st July 1916 TO 31st July 1916.

CONFIDENTIAL.

WAR DIARY.

OF

ASSISTANT DIRECTOR OF VETERINARY SERVICES

1st INDIAN CAVALRY DIVISION

From 1st July 1916   To 31st July 1916.

(Volume 1.)

WAR DIARY or INTELLIGENCE SUMMARY.

(Erase heading not required.)

Army Form C. 2118.

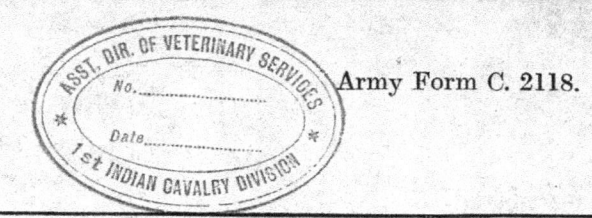

Place	Date	Hour	Summary of Events and Information	Remarks and references to Appendices
DOULLENS	1-7-16		(1) Arranged with R.T.O. for evacuation of sick horses from DOULLENS, but the first batch must not be sent before 4th inst. (2) Made arrangements to evacuate from BOUQUEMAISON until able to use DOULLENS.	
AUXI-LE-CHATEAU	2-7-16		(1) Arranged MHOW Mob. Vet. Sect. to evacuate from BOUQUEMAISON. (2) Division moved at 5.30 P.M. to AUXI-LE-CHATEAU, arrived at 9 P.M. (3) Visited D.D.V.S. 3rd Army. Reported that G.O.C. has given me instructions not to evacuate any more suspicious cases of mange for the time being, owing to the exigencies of the service. (4) SIALKOTE Mob. Vet. Sect. evacuated 18 sick horses.	MAP NO. 11 LENS 1/100,000
"	3-7-16		(1) Arranged with R.T.O. to evacuate sick horses from here (Lucknow & Mhow) Sialkote evacuates from BOUQUEMAISON. (2) Divisional Hd. Qrs. at AUXI-LE-CHATEAU. Sialkote Cav. Bde Hd. Qrs. & M.V.S. REMAISNIL. Lucknow Cav. Bde Hd. Qrs. FROHEN-LE-GRAND. Lucknow Mob. Vet. Sect. FROHEN-LE-PETIT. Mhow Bde Hd. Qrs. & M.V.S. MAIZICOURT. R.H.A. Bde A.Q. & U Batteries, Divisional Ammunition Column WAVANS, BEAUVOIR RIVIERE and NOEUX.	JBMcY

WAR DIARY or INTELLIGENCE SUMMARY.

(Erase heading not required.)

Army Form C. 2118.

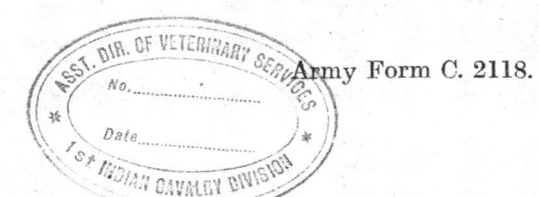

Place	Date	Hour	Summary of Events and Information	Remarks and references to Appendices
AUXI-LE-CHATEAU	4-7-16		(1) Visited A Bty R.H.A. at WAVANS to see suspicious case of mange. Horse no. 62 ordered scrapings to be taken by Capt. R.A. Gooderidge, A.V.C. and horse isolated and dressed. (2) Inspected 3 horses Divisional Hd. Qrs. for mange:- Mr. Rodgy's Ch. G., Lieut. Lang's Br. G. and Police Br. G. (3) Four sick horses of 1st Ind Cavalry Reserve Park evacuated thro' me.	
"	5-7-16		15 sick horses evacuated by MHOW Mob. Vet. Sect.	
"	6-7-16		(1) Visited Field Squadron R.E. to see skin cases and 4 thin horses for evacuation to Rest Farm. Ordered the latter to be sent off at once. (2) 15 sick horses evacuated by Lucknow Mob. Vet. Sect.	
"	7-7-16 & 8-7-16		NIL	
"	9-7-16		18 sick horses evacuated by Sialkote Mob. Vet. Sect.	JaBMcG

WAR DIARY or INTELLIGENCE SUMMARY.

(Erase heading not required.)

Army Form C. 2118.

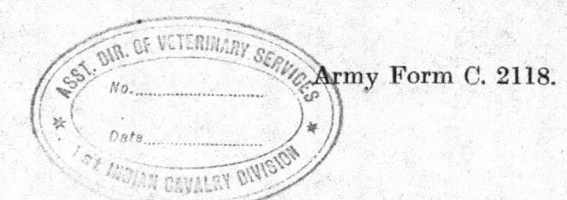

Place	Date	Hour	Summary of Events and Information	Remarks and references to Appendices
AUXI-LE-CHATEAU	10-7-16		(1) Visited D.V.S. re. another v/o for Divisional Troops. He detailed Lieut. F.D. NEAL, A.V.C. to report for duty at once. I reported that I was not evacuating suspicious mange cases under orders from Bde Commander. (2) Farrier Major J. WOOLLEY, reported his departure on duty to 15th Division for training as an Artillery Officer. (3) O.C. Mob. Vet. Sect. Mhow caw. Bde reports collection of B.M. 15.3 star, Socks, B.H. N.F. Coronet from CAFÉ proprietor "N" end of AGENVILLE.	
"	11-7-16		(1) Visited "A" Bty. to see 3 skin cases. Recommended clipping them. (2) Visited Sialkote Machine Gun Squadron to see a Remount suspicious mange case, only joined on the 8th inst. It was very suspicious I ordered B.V.O. (Lieut. Crawford) to take scrapings & report result of examination to me. (3) 20 Sick horses evacuated by MHOW Mob. Vet. Sect. (4) 7 Sick horses " " SIALKOTE " " " (5) 24 " " " " LUCKNOW " " "	JaPMcQ

WAR DIARY or INTELLIGENCE SUMMARY.

(Erase heading not required.)

Army Form C. 2118.

Place	Date	Hour	Summary of Events and Information	Remarks and references to Appendices
AUXI-LE-CHATEAU	12-7-16		(1) Lieut. F.D. NEAL. A.V.C. reported himself for duty with Divisional Troops. (2) 22 sick horses evacuated by Sialkote Mob. Vet. Sect.	
"	13-7-16		(1) Attended Casting Board Lucknow Cav. Bde at FROHEN-LE-GRAND. Ordered 3 cases shewn up as Remount cases to be evacuated as Vety. cases to Convalescent Horse Depôt. (2) Visited Mob. Vet. Sect. Lucknow Cav. Bde. Inspected 4 Debility cases being malleined. Instructed O.C. to keep them under observation for 72 hours before evacuating them. (3) Took over one sick horse suffering from Laminitis from 68th Co. R.E. XI Division. Light Bay Geld. 15.2 aged 7 years (Rider) attached to 1st I.C.D. Field Sqd. R.E. for rations.	
"	14-7-16		(1) Rang up D.V.S. Reported that Lieut. F.D. NEAL, A.V.C., could not ride, consequently was not suitable for Cavalry. D.V.S. asked me to retain the 2 A.V.C. servants and 4 horses for another Vety. officer who he would send up.	JaBMcG

WAR DIARY or INTELLIGENCE SUMMARY.

(Erase heading not required.)

Army Form C. 2118.

Place	Date	Hour	Summary of Events and Information	Remarks and references to Appendices
AUXI LE-CHATEAU.	Continued. 14-7-16		(2) Arranged with D.V.S. to send motor Horse ambulance to collect two sick horses left behind by 67th & 68th Companies R.E. XI Division. (3) Inspected horses of Field Squadron. They are improving in condition. (4) Took over one sick horse suffering from "Wound Contused Kick" inside radius O.F. from 67th Coy: R.E. XI Division. Bay mare 15.2 15 years L.D. attached, for rations to 1st I.C.D. Field Sqdn R.E. (5) Motor ambulance from no. 22 Veterinary Hospital arrived at 6.30 P.M. and evacuated the two sick horses left behind by the 67th & 68th Companies XI Division. (6) Lucknow M.V.S. evacuated one mange case by road. (7) 2 horses of XI Division evacuated by motor ambulance thro: me.	
,,	15-7-16		(1) Lieut: B. PHILP, A.V.C. reported himself for duty with the Division. (2) Lieut: F.D. NEAL, A.V.C. departed for duty in no. 23 Vety: Hospl L. of C. (3) Visited M.V.S. Lucknow Cav: Bde to see suspicious "Reactor" to Eye test with mallein.	ordered

WAR DIARY or INTELLIGENCE SUMMARY.

Army Form C. 2118.

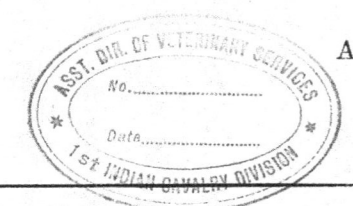

Place	Date	Hour	Summary of Events and Information	Remarks and references to Appendices
AUXI-LE-CHATEAU	Continued 15-7-16		(3) Ordered it to be kept under observation. Saw suspicious mange case of M.V.S. which was also suffering from Chronic lameness (lame after every march) Ordered O.C. M.V.S. to evacuate it. (4) Inspected the Remounts received yesterday by Field Squadron R.E. and found one pronounced case of mange, showing a large patch of 12 inches in diameter on the off side of the neck. I evacuated it into the MHOW M.V.S. and am reporting it to the D.D.V.S and D.D.R. 3rd Army. (5) 27 Sick horses evacuated by MHOW M.V.S. (6) 9 " " " " LUCKNOW "	
,,	16-7-16		(1) Reported (by wire no 828) to D.D.V.S. 3rd Army, one case of mange in Remounts issued to Field Squadron R.E., on Friday 14th inst. at FREVENT Railhead. (Also spoke to D.D.V.S. on phone 7.P.M.) (2) Visited MHOW M.V.S. examined scrapings of mange case in Remount sent in from Field Squadron R.E. yesterday.	

WAR DIARY or INTELLIGENCE SUMMARY.

(Erase heading not required.)

Army Form C. 2118.

Place	Date	Hour	Summary of Events and Information	Remarks and references to Appendices
AUXI-LE-CHATEAU	17-7-16		(1) Attended Casting Board at MHOW Bde. H.Qrs. (MAIZICOURT). Ordered 3 cases of 38th C.I. Horse to be evacuated to Convalescent Horse Depôt. (2) Visited MHOW M.V.S. met D.D.V.S. there we examined scrapings from suspicious case of mange in a Remount sent to Field Sqd. R.E. on the 14th inst. (3) Reported and showed the above case to D.D.R. 3rd Army. (4) Lucknow M.V.S. evacuated one mange case by road.	
"	18-7-16		(1) Wired A.D.V.S. 5th Division to make Vety. arrangements for "U" Bty. R.H.A. now attached to that Division. (2) Visited Lucknow Bde. Hd. Qrs. inspected Major Turner's Charger, which is being dressed for mange. The skin was not quite so irritable as it was. Ordered dressing to be continued. (3) Visited Sialkote M.V.S. inspected 2 suspicious mange cases (Remounts received recently.) Ordered them to be clipped and dressed. Ordered the M.G. Sqd. Remount to be evacuated for mange. (4) The Division leaves AUXI-LE-CHATEAU tomorrow morning 9 A.M. for VILLERS-CHATEL.	H.B.McL

WAR DIARY or INTELLIGENCE SUMMARY.

Army Form C. 2118.

Instructions regarding War Diaries and Intelligence Summaries are contained in F. S. Regs., Part II. and the Staff Manual respectively. Title pages will be prepared in manuscript.

(Erase heading not required.)

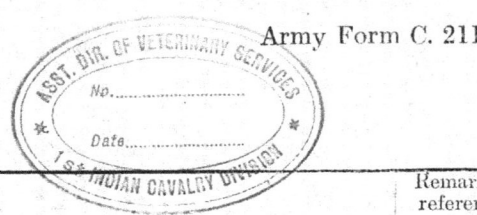

Place	Date	Hour	Summary of Events and Information	Remarks and references to Appendices
AUXI-LE-CHATEAU	Continued 18-7-16		(5) MHOW M.V.S. evacuated 9 sick horses. (6) LUCKNOW " " 11 " " .	
SAVY-BERLETTE	19-7-16		(1) Division moved from AUXI-LE-CHATEAU 9 A.M. and arrived in new area (26 miles march). Divisional Hd. Qrs. VILLERS-CHATEL. (2) Heard of several casualties on the road, but they have not yet been reported. (3) LUCKNOW M.V.S. evacuated 7 sick horses. (4) SIALKOTE " " 1 " horse. (5) MHOW " " 2 " horses.	MAP No. 11 LENS 1/100,000
,,	20-7-16		(1) Visited Divisional Hd. Qrs. at VILLERS-CHATEL. (2) Visited Town MAJOR S.t AUBIGNY re. billets. (3) Capt. R.A. Gooderidge, A.V.C. reported that 4 horses had been left behind in last area, but says he will recover them tomorrow.	

WAR DIARY or INTELLIGENCE SUMMARY.

Army Form C. 2118.

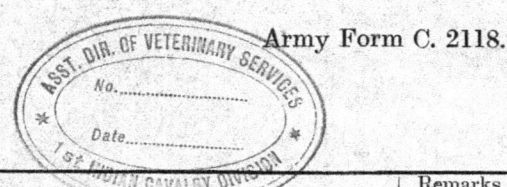

Place	Date	Hour	Summary of Events and Information	Remarks and references to Appendices
SAVY-BERLETTE	Continued 20-7-16		(4) SIALKOTE Bde Hd. Qrs + M.V.S. at AGNEZ-LES-DUISANS. LUCKNOW " " " " " VILLERS-BRULIN. MHOW " " " " " ROELLECOURT. (5) Issued orders for the following:- Lieut. B. PHILP, A.V.C from Auxiliary Horse T. Co. to R.H.A. Bde Capt C.M. BARTON, " to take over Vety charge of Auxiliary H.T. Co. in addition to his present charge Capt H.B. WILLIAMS, " " " " " " of Ambala Fd ambulance " do " P.T. SAUNDERS, " " " " " " of Jodhpur Lancers " do	
"	21-7-16		Visited SIALKOTE M.V.S. instructed O.C. to evacuate sick from AUBIGNY. R.T.O requires 24 hours notice. Train leaves 10. A.M.	
"	22-7-16		(1) Visited Divisional Hd. Qrs re. car to go to 3rd Army Artillery School on Monday, 24th to lecture. (3) Visited Lucknow M.V.S. at BETHENCOURT, where it had just removed to, as there was not enough room in VILLERS-BRULIN. Instructed O.C. M.V.S. to return the Remount Transfers to their units again.	J.B.McQ

WAR DIARY or INTELLIGENCE SUMMARY.

Army Form C. 2118.

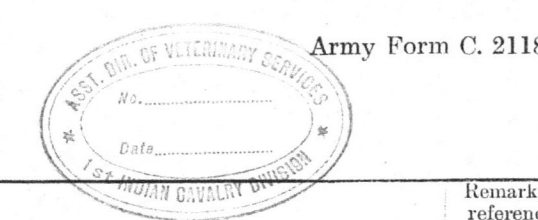

Place	Date	Hour	Summary of Events and Information	Remarks and references to Appendices
SAVY-BERLETTE	Continued 22-7-16		(3) Also arranged to send 4 Shoeing Smiths from Jodhpur Lancers to School of Farriery on 1st August. (These are in addition to the allotment for this Division). D.A.A. + Q.M.G. will arrange for their rations to be sent weekly. (4) Visited Lucknow Cav. Bde. Hd. Qrs reported that I have given orders for Remount Transfers to be sent back to their units who would send them to No.1 Field Remount Section. (5) SIALKOTE M.V.S. evacuated 15 sick horses.	
,,	23-7-16		(1) Capt. W.E. Phipps, A.V.C. took over charge of 36th J. Horse and handed over K.2Go. to Capt P.T. Saunders, A.V.C. (2) MHOW M.V.S. evacuated 11 sick horses.	
,,	24-7-16		(1) Visited 3rd Army Artillery School at HAUTE CLOQUE and lectured to the students from 2 P.M. to 4 P.M. on Veterinary First Aid Treatment etc. (2) LUCKNOW M.V.S. evacuated 12 sick horses.	

WAR DIARY or **INTELLIGENCE SUMMARY.**
(Erase heading not required.)

Army Form C. 2118.

Place	Date	Hour	Summary of Events and Information	Remarks and references to Appendices
SAVY-BERLETTE	25-7-16		(1) Visited Lucknow M.V.S. Inspected men drilled by the new Sergt. just arrived (Sgt. PERRIN) (2) Visited Lucknow Bde. Hd. Qrs. saw B.V.O. re-clipping machines for skin cases. Informed him that A.D.O.S. was issuing 15 pairs of hand clippers to the Bde; and the M.V.S. clippers should be used as much as possible. (3) Visited Lucknow M.G. Sqd. inspected the horses for mange but failed to detect any.	
"	26-7-16		(1) D.D.V.S. notified me that he had a horse suffering from Laminitis at ST: POL for evacuation. (2) Wired to O.C. MHOW M.V.S. instructing him to evacuate one horse suffering from Laminitis at ST: POL. He should apply to D.D.V.S. as to whereabouts of this animal. (3) Visited A.D.V.S. 60th Division at HERMAVILLE re: standings of R.H.A. Bde. in 60th Division area.	

WAR DIARY or INTELLIGENCE SUMMARY

Army Form C. 2118.

Place	Date	Hour	Summary of Events and Information	Remarks and references to Appendices
SAVY-BERLETTE	27/7/16		(1) Lieut. B. PHILP, A.V.C. called and reported that Privates W.T. Walker and J. Allan, A.V.C. had left for no. 23 Veterinary Hospital this morning. (2) Visited Field Squadron R.E. Inspected all the horses. Shoeing was bad. Many cases of Thrush. (3) Visited Divisional Hd. Qrs. Inspected 5 suspicious mange cases which are being dressed with Calcium Sulphide Solution. They seem to be improving. (4) O.C. M.V.S. MHOW Cav. Bde. collected a horse suffering from Laminitis at Remount Stable ST. POL. (5) MHOW M.V.S. evacuated 8 sick horses. (6) SIALKOTE " " 20 " " .	
,,	28/7/16		(1) Capt. A.B. Bowhay, A.V.C. reported that he had collected and evacuated a chestnut horse suffering from Laminitis from the Remount Stable at ST. POL. Also that he had collected Capt. R.A. Goodendge's Grey C.B.G. charger from BERLENCOURT.	

WAR DIARY or INTELLIGENCE SUMMARY.

Army Form C. 2118.

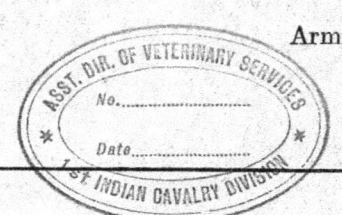

Place	Date	Hour	Summary of Events and Information	Remarks and references to Appendices
SAVY-BERLETTE	Continued 28/7/16		(2) Horse no 246 Q. Bty. R.H.A. left behind sick at WAVANS was collected by no 22 Veterinary Hospital by motor ambulance. (3) Visited Ambala Field ambulance at ACQ HUTS; inspected the suspicious case of mange & ordered it to be evacuated. (4) Visited "A" Bty. R.H.A. at FREVIN-CAPELLE, inspected the 6 suspicious mange cases; and found that the 7th case had been evacuated for Ringbone & nothing mentioned about mange by Lieut. PHILP. A.V.C. Wired to O/C No 22 Vety Hosp.	
"	29/7/16		(1) Visited Divl. Hd. Qrs. Consulted G.O.S. "I" with reference to number of smoke helmets required for horses in this Division now that a large number of horses in the 9th Division have suffered from shell gas. Many of them dying, others had to be destroyed. (2) Visited Lucknow M.V.S. instructed O.C. to evacuate the worst cases of mange. (3) Visited Lucknow Cav. Bde Hd. Qrs. inspected major TURNER's 2nd charger a suspicious mange case. It is being dressed with Calcium Sulphide Solution. (4) MHOW M.V.S. evacuated 8 sick horses.	HRMcG

WAR DIARY or INTELLIGENCE SUMMARY.

(Erase heading not required.)

Army Form C. 2118.

Place	Date	Hour	Summary of Events and Information	Remarks and references to Appendices
SAVY-BERLETTE	30-7-16		(1) Visited A.A.& Q.M.G. and reported that there were well over 100 cases of suspected mange and asked permission to commence evacuating them, as I am afraid of the disease spreading; but the G.O.C. ordered me not to, (owing to the exigencies of the service) (2) Visited 36th Jacob's Horse, inspected 45 suspicious mange cases with Capt PHIPPS, A.V.C. picked out 9 of the worst cases for evacuation. I reported the seriousness of this outbreak to the G.O.C. Bde. and he agreed to my evacuating the worst cases and detailed a Regimental officer to be put entirely in charge of the mange horses, isolated from the rest of the Regiment. (3) O.C. MHOW. M.V.S. collected 2 mules left behind sick at WAVRAN'S by 15th D.A.C. on 25th July. C/o. M. JESSEMINE. DERVAMINE FERME-DE-FERMOISE.	
"	31-7-16		(1) Attended Casting Board with D.D.R. 3rd Army at the Jodhpur Lancers BETHONSART. 9.15 A.M.	

WAR DIARY or INTELLIGENCE SUMMARY.

Army Form C. 2118.

Place	Date	Hour	Summary of Events and Information	Remarks and references to Appendices
SAVY-BERLETTE	Continued 31-7-16		(2) Visited SIALKOTE Mob. Vet. Sect. Inspected suspected mange cases of Brigade :- 17th Lancers - - - 14 and 7 in contacts 19th Lancers - - - 19 6th Cavalry - - - 16 & 1 mule (to be evacuated) M.G. Squadron - - 9 (1 to be evacuated) (3) Visited 17th Lancers. Inspected the animals of Regimental Hd. Qrs for mange. (4) Wired to D.A.D.O.S. to supply Power clipper immediately, Sialkote M.V.S. It had been indented for on 11-7-16. (5) LUCKNOW M.V.S. evacuated 6 sick horses. J.P. McGowan Major A.V.C. A.D.V.S. 1st Indi. Cav. Div.	

SERIAL NO. 322

Confidential War Diary

of

A.D.V.S., 1st Indian Cavalry Division

FROM 1st August 1916 TO 31st August 1916

WAR DIARY or INTELLIGENCE SUMMARY.

(Erase heading not required.)

Army Form C. 2118.

Place	Date	Hour	Summary of Events and Information	Remarks and references to Appendices
SAVY-BERLETTE	1-8-16		(1) Visited A.A. & Q.M.G. re-power clippers being supplied immediately to Sialkote M.V.S. Also Capt. W.E. PHIPPS' transfer.	
			(2) Rang up D.V.S. and asked him for permission to send 2 men from Divisional Police to School of Farriery, which he agreed to. The men leave this evening.	MAP NO: 11 LENS 1/10,000
			(3) Visited 36th Jacob's Horse at VILLERS-BRULIN. Inspected the 45 skin cases which are now under a special regimental officer and are isolated in a field away from the other squadrons.	
			(4) Capt. C.M. BARTON. A.V.C., took over veterinary charge of 1st I.C.D. Reserve Park.	
			(5) Mhow M.V.S. evacuated 8 sick horses.	
,,	2-8-16		(1) Visited A.A. & Q.M.G. for conference on General Gage's Scheme on Friday, 4th and the working of Lucknow M.V.S.	
			(2) Visited Lucknow Machine Gun Squadron. Inspected 3 horses (nos: 213, 87, 332) suspicious mange cases. Ordered no: 87 to be evacuated at once, and the other two to be clipped, also inspected nos: 308, 206, 215	

WAR DIARY or INTELLIGENCE SUMMARY.

(Erase heading not required.)

Army Form C. 2118.

Place	Date	Hour	Summary of Events and Information	Remarks and references to Appendices
SAVY-BERLETTE	Continued 2=8=16		(2) (of the 36th Jacob's Horse Sect.) and nos: 1411, 1414, (of the 29th Lancers Sect.), all of which had been in contact with the suspicious cases. Requested the O.C. to have them clipped and dressed once as soon as possible. Inspected the whole squadron afterwards pointed out the shoeing was very bad.	M.4.S. M.4.S
,,	3=8=16		(1) Visited A.A.& Q.M.G. re: power clippers for each unit with suspicious mange cases. (one each Regiment and one for "A Battery.) (2) Arranged with Divisional Liaison officer to take me to ROELLECOURT and LIGNY-ST-FLOCHEL to see mangey horses belonging to Civilian Frenchmen. (3) Visited Lucknow Machine Gun Sqd., M.V.S., 36th Jacob's Horse and Divl H.Qrs (4) Sialkote M.V.S. evacuated 17 sick horses. Mhow " " 12 " ".	
,,	4=8=16		(1) Field Day, with Lucknow Cavalry Bde; practice working of M.V.S. with B.V.O. in command of British personnel as First Aid and	

WAR DIARY or INTELLIGENCE SUMMARY.

Army Form C. 2118.

Place	Date	Hour	Summary of Events and Information	Remarks and references to Appendices
SAVY-BERLETTE	continued 4/8/16	(1)	and collecting party. Divisional V/O and O.C. M.V.S. with M.V.S. Hd. Qrs. at A.P.M's. Collecting post. I found that the proper place for the A.D.V.S. (myself) to be was at the A.P.M's. Collecting post, where I could see what animals were coming in and give instructions direct.	
		(2)	Visited M. DEBRIL of LIGNY-ST-FLOCHEL and M. FLAMENT cultivateur ROELLECOURT, with Lieut. RAZY, Divisional Liaison Officer to see mangey French horses. We took Capt. A.B. BOWHAY, A.V.C., with us, and arranged to have the two horses dressed by the Mhow M.V.S. Mange notices were put up and the owners warned not to work the horses until they were cured.	
,,	5-8-16	(1)	Arranged with A.A. & Q.M.G. that I would be allowed to send one man from each M.V.S. alternately for one month at a time as a Dresser at Divisional Hd. Qrs. to work under the V/O y/c Divisional troops, and relieve the Shoeing Establishment (who are being overworked at present).	J.W.P. McG

WAR DIARY or INTELLIGENCE SUMMARY

Army Form C. 2118.

(Erase heading not required.)

Place	Date	Hour	Summary of Events and Information	Remarks and references to Appendices
SAVY-BERLETTE	Continued. 5-8-16		(2) Visited Lucknow M.V.S. Instructed O.C. to arrange for an N.C.O. or a reliable British soldier to always be present in the Section Lines when the O.C. was not there. (3) Visited B.V.O. Lucknow Cav. Bde. and 29th Lancers to see mange cases for evacuation, but most of the animals were out. I saw two and ordered B.V.O. to evacuate them.	
"	6-8-16		(1) Visited Divisional Hd. Qrs. re-distribution of work among the Farriery Establishment of Hd. Qrs. Signals and A.S.C. Also reported that the Interpreter attached to me (as A.D.V.S.) had been transferred and another one had not been detailed in his place. (2) Lucknow M.V.S. evacuated 20 sick horses. Mhow " " 8 " " .	

WAR DIARY or INTELLIGENCE SUMMARY.

(Erase heading not required.)

Army Form C. 2118.

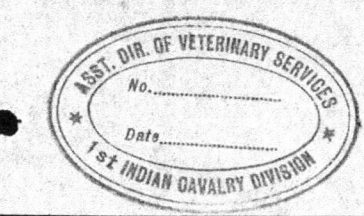

Place	Date	Hour	Summary of Events and Information	Remarks and references to Appendices
SAVY-BERLETTE	7-8-16		(1) D.D.V.S. called at office. We visited the Lucknow M.V.S. at BETHENCOURT and the 29th Lancers at CHELERS where we inspected the 50 horses which are being dressed for skin disease. Also inspected 8 cases of the 1st K.D. Guards, 6 of which we ordered to be evacuated.	
do	8-8-16		(1) Visited A.A. & Q.M.G. re. instructions given to B.V.O. Lucknow Cav. Bde. about mange cases in 29th Lancers in the presence of the Adjutant of the Regiment. The mange cases were not isolated from the Squadrons and the Regimental officer was not put in sole charge. He was apparently doing other regimental duties. (2) Visited Lucknow M.V.S. met D.D.V.S. there and discussed the question of Capt. W.E. PHIPPS' transfer from this Division. D.D.V.S. said he would place the matter before D.V.S. Supervised the dressing of 40 suspicious mange cases and in contacts of the 36th Jacob's Horse with Calcium Sulphide Solution. (3) Private WARHAM, A.V.C. returned to M.V.S. from Divisional Hd. Qrs. and	

WAR DIARY or INTELLIGENCE SUMMARY.

(Erase heading not required.)

Army Form C. 2118.

Place	Date	Hour	Summary of Events and Information	Remarks and references to Appendices
SAVY-BERLETTE	Continued 8-8-16		(3) and was replaced by no: S.E. 5866 Pte. H. Page A.V.C. who will do one month's duty under V/O i/c Divisional Troops as a Dresser, at the end of the month he will be replaced by another man from another M.V.S. (4) Lucknow M.V.S. evacuated 10 sick horses.	
,,	9-8-16		(1) Sent in to A.A. + Q.M.G. my report on working of A.V.S. with Lucknow Cavalry Brigade Scheme on 4.8.16. (2) Reported to A.A. + Q.M.G. that a box of very light Indian or Egyptian horse shoes with thin drawn out rolled toes had been issued to the Jodhpur Lancers. In my opinion they would wear out in 8 or 9 days with ordinary exercise work. (3) Recommended the A.A. + Q.M.G. to advise that all horses in the Division should be billeted in the open owing to the large number of glanders and mange infected billets in the Divisional billeting area. (4) Lucknow Machine Gun Squadron left one horse (suffering from an extensive lacerated wound in the pectoral region) with MADAME HORN at HELIN-LE-VERT. Horse Recovery Farm no. 1 was handed over.	JAPMcG (5)

WAR DIARY or INTELLIGENCE SUMMARY.

(Erase heading not required.)

Army Form C. 2118.

Instructions regarding War Diaries and Intelligence Summaries are contained in F. S. Regs., Part II. and the Staff Manual respectively. Title pages will be prepared in manuscript.

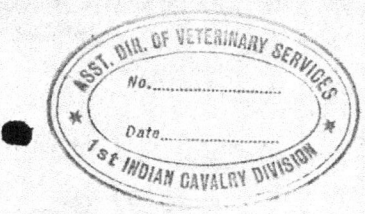

Place	Date	Hour	Summary of Events and Information	Remarks and references to Appendices
SAY-BERLETTE	Continued 9-8-16		(5) Lucknow Cavalry Bde: joined 7th Corps and moved to:- Bde. Hd. Qrs. at PAS, 1st K.D. Guards at HUMBERCOURT, 29th Lancers at WARLUZEL, 36th Jacob's Horse at COULLEMONT and Mobile Vety. Sect: at COUTURELLE. (6) Sialkote M.V.S. evacuated 11 sick horses. Mhow " " 8 " "	
,,	10-8-16		(1) I accompanied the Liaison Officer French mission 1st I.C.D. to see 2 horses suffering from mange, owned by French Civilian in the Divisional billeting area at:- NO:I MADAME JULES-FINET (next door to no. 5 Billet) BAILLEUL-AUX-CORNAILLES. 1 Bay foal 10 months old affected practically all over. NO:II M. ALEXIS-NICHOLAS, Farmer, HERLIN-LE-VERT. 1 white cart mare 10 years, only very slightly affected on the withers. The instructions in the French Decree were carried out. (2) Visited MADAME HORN at HERLIN-LE-VERT, to see the sick horse left behind by Lucknow M.G. Sqd: yesterday. Whilst I was there the Horse ambulance from no. 21 M.V.S. 9th Infantry Division arrived and took it away.	

WAR DIARY or INTELLIGENCE SUMMARY

Army Form C. 2118.

Place	Date	Hour	Summary of Events and Information	Remarks and references to Appendices
SAVY-BERLETTE	Continued 10-8-16		(3) Rendered list to D.D.V.S. of horses (by units) in this Division, being dressed as suspected mange (Copy in Mange File) (4) Found a pony about 18 years old suffering from Laminitis left behind on the 15th July by a Scotch Regiment which was passing through BAILLEUL-AUX-CORNAILLES. I ordered its destruction, which was carried out by the A.V.C. Sergeant serving under Lieut: O. PLUNKETT, No: 3 Section, 21st Reserve Park. (5) Mhow Cavalry Bde: marched into new billets :- Bde. Hd. Qrs., 38th C.I.H., M.G. Sqd. and M.V.S. at CAMBLIGNEUL, 6th Inniskilling Dragoons at PENIN, and 2nd Lancers at MONTS-EN-TERNOIS.	
,,	11-8-16		(1) Visited (with A.A. & Q.M.G.) the 29th Lancers, 36th Jacob's Horse and Bde. Hd. Qrs. at P.4.S. Inspected all the suspicious mange cases. Ordered one of the 36th J. Horse to be evacuated, sent 13 others back to duty. (2) Brought the centrefuge back from Lucknow M.V.S. (3) Capt. R.A. GOODERIDGE, took over vety. charge of 1st I.C.D. Reserve Park and Auxiliary H.T. Coy. (4) Capt. C.M. BARTON, took over veterinary charge of Sialkote Cavalry Field Ambulance at TINQUES.	JasMcy

WAR DIARY or INTELLIGENCE SUMMARY.

Army Form C. 2118.

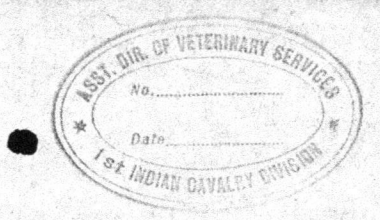

Place	Date	Hour	Summary of Events and Information	Remarks and references to Appendices
SAVY-BERLETTE	12-8-16		(1) Visited Mahow M.V.S. to inspect 6 suspicious mange cases of the 38th C.I.H. Ordered them to be clipped, dressed and evacuated. Reported these cases to D.A.V.S. by wire no 864 of today.	
			(2) Forwarded and recommended application of No. 121 Sergt. J. Smith, A.V.C. to rank of Staff Sergeant.	
			(3) Inspected 35 skin cases in Jodhpur Lancers :- 5 Infected (1 for evacuation), 8 slightly affected, 8 very slightly affected, 14 Itchy but no signs of lesions.	
			(4) Applied to A.A.+Q.M.G. to inform V/O i/c Divisional Troops when remounts were expected, and he would inspect them at Railhead.	
			(5) Notified A.A.+Q.M.G. and all Vety Officers that cases of an "influenza type" of catarrhal Fever had occurred and asked for a Divisional order to be published recommending immediate isolation of all Fever and catarrh cases and report to Vety Officer incharge of the unit.	
			(6) Lucknow M.V.S. evacuated 6 sick horses.	

WAR DIARY or INTELLIGENCE SUMMARY.

(Erase heading not required.)

Army Form C. 2118.

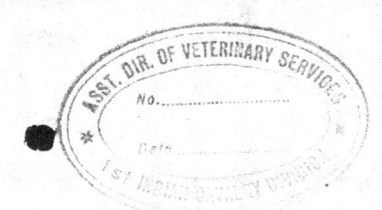

Place	Date	Hour	Summary of Events and Information	Remarks and references to Appendices
SAVY-BERLETTE	13-8-16		(1) Notified A.A. & Q.M.G. and all Veterinary officers in the Division that a few cases of an "Influenza type of Catarrhal Fever" had occurred, and advised immediate isolation of animals with Fever and nasal discharge or cough, and disinfection of all nose bags.	
			(2) B.V.O. Mhow Cav. Bde. reported that he had condemned the water supply of PENIN where the 6th Inniskilling Dragoons are billeted.	
			(3) Reported to D.D.V.S. 5 suspicious mange cases in the Jodhpur Lancers.	
			(4) Mhow M.V.S. evacuated 15 sick horses.	
,,	14-8-16		(1) Wrote out special report for D.D.V.S. on the duties of an A.D.V.S. with a Cavalry Division.	
			(2) Attended a conference with 'Q' staff at Divisional Hd. Qrs. at 6.30 P.M. Discussed the working of the 3 M.V. Sections in conjunction with Senior Supply Officer.	
			(3) Got the sanction for 6 maps to be issued to each for Mobile Veterinary Sections.	

WAR DIARY or INTELLIGENCE SUMMARY.

(Erase heading not required.)

Army Form C. 2118.

Place	Date	Hour	Summary of Events and Information	Remarks and references to Appendices
SAVY-BERLETTE	15=8=16		(1) Rendered report on Duties of an A.D.V.S. with Cavalry Division to D.D.V.S. asked for by D.V.S. (2) Wired to all Veterinary Officers to send "Progress Reports" on outbreaks of mange, according to my memo: no.1202 dated 13.8.16.	
,,	16=8=16		(1) Lieut. B. PHILP, applied for leave from 19th to 27th. I forwarded and recommended him for 7 days only to D.D.V.S. (2) Received telephonic message from D.V.S. that Capt. P.D. CAREY, A.V.C. would take over Lucknow M.V.S. from Capt. W.E. PHIPPS, A.V.C. in a day or two, and that Lieut. J.H. CRAWFORD, A.V.C. B.V.O. Sialkote Cavalry Brigade would be replaced by Lieut. C.C. PARSONS. (3) Notification received from D.V.S. that a Horse Float had been sanctioned for the 1st I.C.D. and that it would be ready for collection in about two weeks time. (4) Inspected 5 suspicious mange cases at Divisional Headquarters. Discharged Capt. HAZELTINE'S, chestnut charger for duty, the	

WAR DIARY or INTELLIGENCE SUMMARY.

Army Form C. 2118.

Place	Date	Hour	Summary of Events and Information	Remarks and references to Appendices
SAVY-BERLETTE	Continued 16-8-16		(4) The other 4 cases are yielding to treatment and will soon be ready for duty. (5) Mhow M.V.S. evacuated 14 sick horses. Lucknow " " 26 " "	
"	17-8-16		(1) Visited G.O.C. Lucknow Cavalry Bde, re: suspicious mange cases. (2) Visited and inspected all animals in the 1st K.D. Guards at HUMBERCOURT, picked out 3 suspicious mange cases, which with the 5 previous cases made a total of 8 suspicious cases which are isolated now in a separate field. (3) Visited and inspected all animals Lucknow M.G. Sqd. at HUMBERCOURT. Saw 7 suspicious mange cases and one "in contact case". Recommended isolation, clipping, good grooming and keeping under observation for a few days.	
"	18-8-16		(1) Inspected horses of Jodhpur Lancers. Ordered 4 horses and 1 mule to be evacuated and 5 cases to be isolated as suspicious cases of mange.	

WAR DIARY or INTELLIGENCE SUMMARY.

Army Form C. 2118.

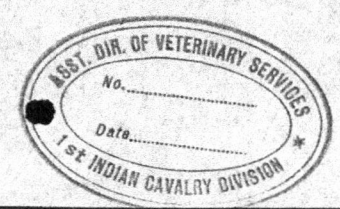

Place	Date	Hour	Summary of Events and Information	Remarks and references to Appendices
SAVY-BERLETTE	Continued. 18-8-16		(1) Fifteen animals were put into working isolation as they had been in contact with suspicious mange cases.	
			(2) Received instructions from D.D.V.S. to evacuate sick of 1st I.C.D. Reserve Park and Auxiliary H.T. Co. into no.50 M.V.S. 39th Division at LE QUESNEL.	
			(3) Issued orders to Capt. W.E. PHIPPS, A.V.C. to proceed to No. 5 Veterinary Hospital ABBEVILLE, on relief by Capt. P.D. CAREY, A.V.C. See Telegram no. 878.	
			(4) Forwarded Lieut. B. PHILP'S application for leave from 21st to 27th August on urgent private affairs. D.D.V.S. approved of it.	
			(5) Rendered report to D.D.V.S. on working of A.V.C. in this Division under the headings in D.D.V.S. circular memo no. 5 of 31.7.16.	
			(6) Capt. P.D. CAREY, A.V.C. reported himself for duty with the M.V.S. Lucknow Cav. Bde.	
			(7) Sialkote M.V.S. evacuated 11 sick horses. Mhow " " 8 " "	

WAR DIARY or INTELLIGENCE SUMMARY.

(Erase heading not required.)

Army Form C. 2118.

Place	Date	Hour	Summary of Events and Information	Remarks and references to Appendices
SAVY-BERLETTE	19-8-16		(1) Visited 29th Lancers at WARLINCOURT. Inspected every animal in the Regiment for mange. The suspicious mange cases now under treatment are recovering. I ordered Capt. P.T. SAUNDERS to discontinue dressing all except 3, but keep them close clipped well groomed and under observation. (2) Visited 36th Jacob's Horse at GAUDIEMPRE. Inspected every animal in the Regiment for mange. I ordered one horse to be evacuated. All the suspicious cases and incontacts are recovering. There are only 15 being dressed now. Over 20 cases have been selected for being discharged to duty, but are being kept under observation and well groomed for a few more days. (3) Capt. A.B. BOWHAY, A.V.C. took over veterinary charge of the no. 278th Railway Company R.E. at CAMBLIGNEUL. (4) Capt. W.E. PHIPPS, A.V.C. handed over M.V.S. Lucknow Cav. Bde. to Capt. P.D. CAREY, A.V.C. and left this Division for duty at N° 5 Veterinary Hospital ABBEVILLE.	JaRMcQ

WAR DIARY or INTELLIGENCE SUMMARY.

(Erase heading not required.)

Army Form C. 2118.

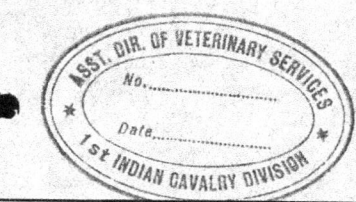

Place	Date	Hour	Summary of Events and Information	Remarks and references to Appendices
SAVY-BERLETTE	20-8-16		(1) Compiled and forwarded to D.D.V.S. a progress report on the outbreak of mange in the different units in the 1st Indian Cavalry Division.	
			(2) Forwarded to Lieut. B. PHILP. his leave, sanctioned from 22nd to 28th August. Asked him to report his departure and give me his home address.	
			(3) Capt. W.E. PHIPPS. A.V.C. reports his departure on leave to Ireland, after which he joins no. 5 Veterinary Hospital ABBEVILLE for duty.	
			(4) Mohow M.V.S. evacuated 4 sick horses.	
"	21-8-16		(1) Inspected 17 Remounts for the Division at Railhead (TINQUES) and found 4 with a nasal discharge. I labelled them for isolation and gave instructions for them to be shown to the Vety. officer in charge.	
			(2) Rang up D.V.S. re. Horse Float for the Division and he promised to provide a horse and harness for the float and will let me know when to send for it.	
			(3) D.V.S. has sanctioned the temporary attachment of an A.V.C. Sergeant to the Auxiliary Horse Transport Co. 1st I.C.D., but he has not joined yet.	
			(4) Lucknow M.V. Section moved from HAUTBAIS FARM to COUTURELLE.	J.P.McG

(5)

WAR DIARY or INTELLIGENCE SUMMARY.

(Erase heading not required.)

Army Form C. 2118.

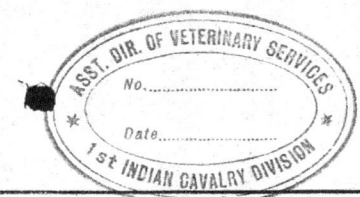

Place	Date	Hour	Summary of Events and Information	Remarks and references to Appendices
SAVY-BERLETTE	Continued 21-8-16		(5) Inspected the horses and mules of the Sialkote Cavalry Field Ambulance at TINQUETTE. They were in good condition and well shod.	
,,	22-8-16		(1) O.C. M.V.S. Lucknow Cav. Bde. reported that the field in which the M.V. Section is now billeted has been used for standing mange cases. He has disinfected the area with lime.	
			(2) Visited A.A. & Q.M.G to find out what units 3 Remounts from No. 11 Squadron No. 1 Base Remount Depôt ROUEN had been posted to, as a dangerous clinical case of Glanders in a horse which belonged to the same Squadron had occurred since they left ROUEN. I sent instructions to all Veterinary officers to test all remounts in the units in their Veterinary charge which had been received on the July 28th, August 4th & 14th and report results to me as soon as possible (see my urgent memo to all V/o's no. 1228 d/22-8-16).	
			(3) Interpreter M-de-L D'ISLE reported himself for duty with A.D.V.S. I attached him to Sialkote M.V.S.	JaBMcl
			(4) Lucknow M.V.S. evacuated 12 sick horses.	

WAR DIARY or INTELLIGENCE SUMMARY.

(Erase heading not required.)

Army Form C. 2118.

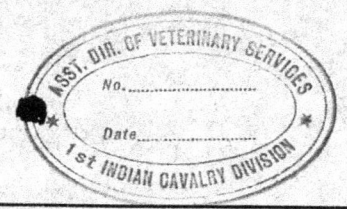

Instructions regarding War Diaries and Intelligence Summaries are contained in F. S. Regs., Part II. and the Staff Manual respectively. Title pages will be prepared in manuscript.

Place	Date	Hour	Summary of Events and Information	Remarks and references to Appendices
SAVY-BERLETTE	23-8-16		(1) Inspected all horses in "A" Bty. R.H.A. at FREVIN-CAPELLE for mange. The 7 cases isolated under observation are doing very well, all irritation having disappeared and the skins are soft and coats coming. (2) D.V.S. rang me up and asked me if I recommended Capt. A. HORNER. A.V.C. for the appointment of the 8th Division, which I did. D.V.S. asked me to send him my scheme for the working of M.V. Sections in this Division. (3) Lieut. C.C. PARSONS. A.V.C. reported himself as B.V.O. Sialkote Cav. Bde.	
,,	24-8-16		(1) Lieut. C.C. PARSONS. A.V.C. called and reported that he had taken over as B.V.O. Sialkote Cav. Bde from Lieut. J.H. CRAWFORD. A.V.C. (2) Inspected all animals in 38th C.I.H. for mange at CAMBLIGNEUL, discovered 1 suspicious case (Lieut. WOODHOUSE's Batman's horse). Ordered to be isolated and dressed with Calcium Sulphide Solution. The shoeing in this regiment is bad, and they are not using the tilted toe shoe; I instructed Capt. A.B. BOWHAY. A.V.C. to give	J.R.M.

WAR DIARY or INTELLIGENCE SUMMARY.

Army Form C. 2118.

Place	Date	Hour	Summary of Events and Information	Remarks and references to Appendices
SAVY-BERLETTE	Continued 24-8-16		(2) give demonstrations in the forges on the making and use of the Tilted toe shoe, also to point out the many faults in the shoeing of this regiment. (3) Inspected the men and horses of Mhow M.V.S.	
"	25-8-16		(1) Sent in my report to G.O.C. Mhow Cav. Bde on inspection of the 38th C.I.H. for mange. Reported that the outbreak was now under control, that the shoeing was bad, that the tilted toe shoe was not in use, also that a nailbound had been sent to the trenches. (2) Inspected animals of the Mhow M.G. Sqd. Ordered several itchy horses to be clipped. Horses were in good condition. The Tilted toe shoe was not in use in this unit. (3) Applied to G.O.C. Mhow Cav. Bde for permission to inspect the 2nd Lancers at MONTS-EN-TERNOIS tomorrow. (4) Lieut. J.H. CRAWFORD, A.V.C. left for England on the expiration of his contract with Government, his address c/o Messrs GRINDLAY & Co. 54 Parliament Street, London S.W.	

WAR DIARY or INTELLIGENCE SUMMARY.

(Erase heading not required.)

Army Form C. 2118.

Place	Date	Hour	Summary of Events and Information	Remarks and references to Appendices
SAVY-BERLETTE	26-8-16		(1) Inspected 2nd Lancers at MONTS-EN-TERNOIS. All animals were in good condition with the exception of 9 horses which had been overdressed with too strong Calcium Sulphide Solution. The shoeing is not good as the clinches are too low in the wall and do not get sufficient grip of the horn. (2) Mhow M.V.S. evacuated 8 sick horses.	
"	27-8-16		(1) Received telegram from Lieut. B. PHILP. A.V.C, saying that he had been placed on the sick list at 108 South Street ST. ANDREWS, saying that he had written and was sending medical certificate. (2) Reported to D.D.V.S. 3rd Army that Lieut B. PHILP. had been reported sick at his home in SCOTLAND. (3) Completed scheme for working of Army Veterinary Services in an Indian Cavalry Division for the D.V.S. (4) Lucknow M.V.S. evacuated 7 sick horses.	JaSmey

WAR DIARY or INTELLIGENCE SUMMARY

Army Form C. 2118.

(Erase heading not required.)

Place	Date	Hour	Summary of Events and Information	Remarks and references to Appendices
SAVY-BERLETTE	28-8-16		(1) Interviewed G.S.O.2. Division re Scheme for working of M.V. Sections in an Indian Cavalry Division, left the scheme with him until tomorrow. (2) Sialkote M.V.S. evacuated 13 sick horses.	
"	29-8-16		(1) Applied to A.A. & Q.M.G. for Farrier Major ARNOLD, 17th Lancers to be detailed for temporary duty at Divisional Hd. Qrs. as Lieut. B. PHILP, had reported sick whilst on leave in Scotland. (2) Forwarded the back numbers of all circular memos to Capt P.D. CAREY, A.V.C. and Lieut. C.C. PARSONS, for information, guidance and return.	
"	30-8-16		(1) Arranged with A.A. & Q.M.G. to supply vety officer i/c Divisional Troops with an "arrow" branding iron and that he will brand all animals in the Division which require it. (2) Inspected "B" Squadron 6th Inniskilling Dragoons at PENIN for contagious disease. It rained heavily and the horses were covered in mud so I had to postpone the inspection of remainder until Tuesday 3rd Sept.	JaMe

WAR DIARY or INTELLIGENCE SUMMARY.

(Erase heading not required.)

Army Form C. 2118.

Place	Date	Hour	Summary of Events and Information	Remarks and references to Appendices
SAVY-BERLETTE	30-8-16	Continued	(3) Inspected all Veterinary Equipment of the 6th Inniskilling Dragoons and found everything satisfactory.	
"	31-8-16		(1) Reconstructed the Scheme for working Mobile Veterinary Sections in the Division in accordance with General Officer's Commanding wishes.	

J.R. McGowan
Major A.V.C.
A.D.V.S.
1st Ind. Cav. Divn

SERIAL NO. 322

Confidential
War Diary
of

A.D.V.S. 1st Indian Cavalry Division

FROM 1st September 1916 TO 30th September 1916

WAR DIARY or INTELLIGENCE SUMMARY

Army Form C. 2118.

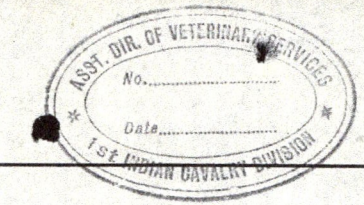

Place	Date	Hour	Summary of Events and Information	Remarks and references to Appendices
S. RIQUIER	4.9.16		Took over from Major J.A.B. McGowan the duties of A.D.V.S. 1st I.C.D. Division marched from FROHEN-LE-GRAND to S. RIQUIER.	
"	5.9.16		CAPT. P.T Saunders AVC proceeded to UK on leave (urgent private affairs) 5.9.16 to 12.9.16. Instructed OC's Mob Vet Sections to evacuate sick animals from S. RIQUIER, but most cases were marched to ABBEVILLE by road (distance about 6 miles).	
"	6.9.16		Inspected Suspicious Mange cases of Lucknow Cav Bde about 60 cases in all; sent 45 to duty as "free from disease" & Kept remaining 15 in isolation as suspicious.	
"	7.9.16		Inspected Suspicious Mange cases of Mhow Cav Bde, about 30 in all. Discharged 20, Kept 10 in isolation as suspicious.	
"	8.9.16		Field day on cavalry training area. Lucknow & Mhow M.V.S. took part. Sent out patrol parties behind APM's stragglers patrols, to look for casualties. Found the ground covered by cavalry too extensive for my patrol parties to be of much use, & formed opinion that it is better to wait until actual information of casualties are in a certain area is received & then send out a party to collect them.	
"	9.9.16		Visited No 5 Veterinary Hospital Abbeville, & saw Mange cases with OC Hospital, also the acarus under microscope etc.	R.A.L.

WAR DIARY or INTELLIGENCE SUMMARY

Army Form C. 2118.

Place	Date	Hour	Summary of Events and Information	Remarks and references to Appendices
ST RIQUIER	11.9.16		Division marched to DOULLENS. Attended a Conference of ADVS' at 4th Army HQ, on "the most suitable method of using MVS during cavalry operations". The conference came to the following conclusions:- ① It is necessary to work M.V.S. on a Divisional Basis. ② Two Sections will move with Divisional "A" Echelon, lightly equipped, & with transport confined to one Limber Wagon each. ③ One section will remain at Railhead or with "B" Echelon, whichever is further advanced. ④ The functions of "A" Echelon Mobile Veterinary Sections are to act as a collecting & clearing Centre for the whole division. ⑤ The functions of the rear M.V.S are to clear the concentration area, to collect from the advanced Sections & despatch to L of C. ⑥ For the ADVS of the Division to properly co-ordinate these duties, he should be with "A" Echelon. The following additional conclusions were arrived at & may be added in amplification of the propositions put forward:- The chain of responsibility for the Veterinary Service with Cavalry assuming its proper rôle may be stated as follows:- ① The Brigade VO or Officers working with the regimental staffs are responsible (for)	

WAR DIARY or INTELLIGENCE SUMMARY

Army Form C. 2118.

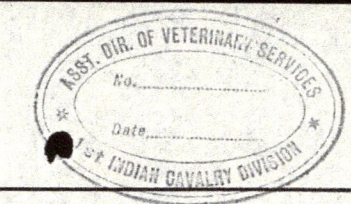

Place	Date	Hour	Summary of Events and Information	Remarks and references to Appendices
			for the rendition of first aid & will decide on the important question of the destruction or retention of seriously injured cases. They will either send the cases into the "A" Echelon M.V.S. or collect them in a suitable position & inform the M.V.S. where they are. (2) The A Echelon M.V. Sections receive the casualties sent in from the units or BVO's & collect any whose position may be notified. Horses will be evacuated from these, either by parties sent down from these sections or by parties sent up from the rear M.V.S., chiefly the latter. (3) The rear M.V.S. or Railhead Section will collect & receive cases from the Advanced M.V.S., holding such until they can arrange for their evacuation to the L of C. It is possible they may have to hold large numbers of horses sometimes for several days. (4) The Divisional V.O. will be with the Divl Troops, especially the Artillery, which quite likely may be Brigaded. The positions occupied by these links in the chain are as follows:- (a) The BVO's with the Bde A Echelon transport. This consists of S.A.A. carts, water carts etc. (b) The A Echelon M.V.S. with the Divl "A" Echelon. (c) The "B" Echelon or rear M.V.S. at Railhead or "B" Echelon, whichever is further advanced. (d) The ADVS with Divl/A Echelon. (e) The D.V.O. with Divl A Echelon or the Amm. Column. While the above organisation was considered the most suitable for any forward role of cavalry, the conclusion was come to that for any (outflanking)	R.A.G.

WAR DIARY or INTELLIGENCE SUMMARY

Army Form C. 2118.

Place	Date	Hour	Summary of Events and Information	Remarks and references to Appendices
			outflanking movement, such as occurred after the battle of the AISNE M.V.S act best by working in the rear of its Brigade, that is the same organisation as is adopted in billets. (Sd. E.E Martin. Col. D.D.V.S 4th Army).	
S. RIQUIER	13.9.16		Division marched from DOULLENS to ALLONVILLE.	
ALLONVILLE	15.9.16	5 AM	Division marched at 5am to bivouacs around MORLANCOURT. B Echelons were left behind but M.V. Sections & their transport marched with A Echelon which was divisionalised & joined up with their respective Brigades at the end of the march.	
	16.9.16		Arranged to evacuate all sick through Lucknow M.V.S, which would act as the Rear M.V.S. in the event of a move forward.	
	17.9.16		Went towards ALBERT (Divisional Railhead) & found a suitable site for the Rear M.V.S. if we move forward. Site was in area E 10 d (Ref Map ALBERT 57 c) & 3 Railheads were available, all within about 3 miles.: EDGE HILL, GROVE TOWN & ALBERT.	
	19.9.16		1 NCO & 9 PRIVATES (AVC) dismounted arrived from No 19 Hospital ROUEN, to act as Conducting Parties to L of C. They were attached to LUCKNOW M.V.S	
	20.9.16		Inspected 6 Remounts of Div. Amm Column, which the C.O. had complained of, as being unfit; found 2 had slight Ringworm & 1 slightly lame, but all were fit for duty within 3 days.	
	21.9.16		Attended conference at Div HQ on forthcoming cavalry operations. Arranged that SIALKOT M.V.S & MHOW M.V.S. should go forward with "A" Echelon	

WAR DIARY or INTELLIGENCE SUMMARY

Army Form C. 2118.

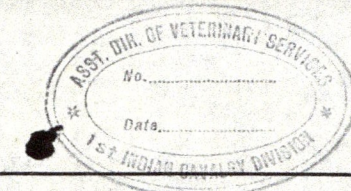

Place	Date	Hour	Summary of Events and Information	Remarks and references to Appendices
			Echelon, but LUCKNOW M.V.S. would remain behind as Rear MVS as the LUCKNOW BDE was in reserve & not moving for the present.	
	25.9.16		Division HQ, MHOW & SIALKOT BDES moved forward to MAMETZ. ~~Sialkot~~ & MHOW MVS also moved up to this place, & SIALKOT MVS remained behind with orders to be ready to move up at an hour's notice if required. Cavalry did not go into action & Division moved back to MORLANCOURT at 8 p.m.	
	27.9.16		DIVISION moved to bivouacs at BUSSY-DAOURS.	
	28.9.16		" " " PICQUIGNY.	
	29.9.16		" " " AILLY-le-HAUT CLOCHER. Lieut PHILP AVC evacuated sick with SCABIES.	
	30.9.16		" " " LIGESCOURT.	

R.A. Goodenough. Capt AVC
ADVS. 1st Ind Cav. Div.

SERIAL NO. 322

Confidential
War Diary
of

A.D.V.S., 4th Cavalry Division (late 1st Ind. Cavy. Divn.)

FROM 1st October 1916 TO 30th November / 31st October 1916

WAR DIARY or INTELLIGENCE SUMMARY

(Erase heading not required.)

Army Form C. 2118.

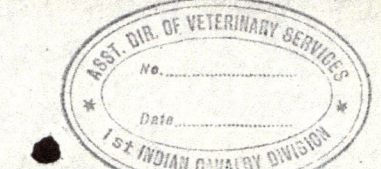

Place	Date	Hour	Summary of Events and Information	Remarks and references to Appendices
LIGESCOURT	1.10.16.		Rode round Divisional Area & saw billets of the 3 Mobile Vety. Sections, they were all well situated for their Brigades. DVS wrote asking where to send Horse-float which is to be attached to the Division, replied, asking for it to be sent to Divisional HQ.	
WADICOURT	2.10.16		ADMS & ADVS moved billets to WADICOURT about 1½ from Div HQ.	
"	3.10.16.		Visited DDVS. CAV.CORPS. & arranged for M.V.S.' to evacuate by road to ABBEVILLE as long as OC's Hospitals could take the horses in. All cases evacuated by rail go to No 7 Hospital. FORGES. LES EAUX. Horse-float arrived for the Division.	Rely
"	4.10.16		Inspected 12 horses of the Wireless Station attached Signal Squadron Div HQ. Found them very poor, & 7 required evacuating for Debility. Reported this to AA.& QMG. Attended Casting Parade with DDR. CAV CORPS at LUCKNOW CAV BDE.	
	5.10.16.		Visited Div HQ Forge & saw two men of the APM Establishment at work shoeing; these men had done a course of Cold Shoeing at School of Farriery. ABBEVILLE, both men showed a good knowledge of shoeing & were good workmen.	
	6.10.16	10.a.m	LT. H.W. STEVENS AVC. arrived from No 1 Hospital to take over Div Troops vice LT PHILO who was sent sick 29.9.16. Inspected horses of Div HQ. Visited Sialkot M.V.S & examined a skin scraping under the microscope & found an acarus, very much resembling the Forage Acarus Type. Arranged to inspect the animal from which the scraping was taken.	

WAR DIARY or ~~INTELLIGENCE SUMMARY~~

(Erase heading not required.)

Army Form C. 2118.

Instructions regarding War Diaries and Intelligence Summaries are contained in F. S. Regs., Part II. and the Staff Manual respectively. Title Pages will be prepared in manuscript.

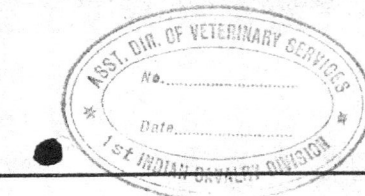

Place	Date	Hour	Summary of Events and Information	Remarks and references to Appendices
WADICOURT	7.10.16		Visited 19th Lancers & saw the suspected Mange case, there were very slight lesions (eruptions) on the neck & withers, ordered the animal to be evacuated. This was the horse from which an acarus was found in a scraping on 6th inst. Examined 4 mules attached to Signal Sqd. of which the O.C. had complained were unfit for work & jibbed. Found 1 to be slightly lame, & ordered him to be returned to a slow moving Unit, the other 3 were good mules & go well when well driven, but the drivers were new & inexperienced.	
" "	9.10.16		Inspected Remounts that had arrived for Div HQ. Signal Squadron, one Ride of latter unit was lame & skin looked unhealthy, ordered him to be clipped & isolated for further inspection. Visited MHOW M.V.S. CAPT BARTON AVC. returned from leave in United Kingdom.	
" "	10.10.16		OC. LUCKNOW MOB. VET. SECTION reported that he had reverted ACTING SERGEANT PERRIN AVC to rank of Private, owing to his inefficiency & also being found in a CAFÉ after closing hours & in charge of a man who was supposed to be "confined to Camp". Also 3 men doing, 14. 21. & 28 days, F.P. No 1, & two men gone to hospital sick. I wired the DDVS Cav. Corps to apply for 5 men to replace these casualties temporarily. Also applied through DDVS. CAV CORPS for ACTING CORPORAL FAULKNER AVC & PTE AMOR AVC to be promoted ACTING SGT & ACTING CORPORAL respectively to fill up the vacancies caused by SGT PERRIN'S reversion. Telephoned DDVS. Cav Corps re keeping both LT. PHILP & LT STEVENS AVC with Divisional Troops & received permission to keep them for the next few weeks.	

WAR DIARY or INTELLIGENCE SUMMARY

Army Form C. 2118.

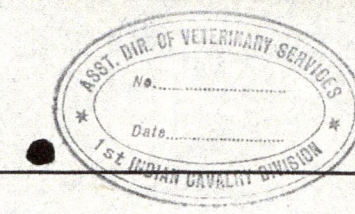

Place	Date	Hour	Summary of Events and Information	Remarks and references to Appendices
WADICOURT	11.10.16		Recommended Capt. H.B. Williams A.V.C. for a Mention in Despatches. O.C. Lucknow Cav Bde. Mob. Vet. Section recommended K. Duffadar IMDAD ALI (29th Lancers) for a reward for constant good work & devotion to duty. 29th Lancers reported not having any trained Saluties in the regiment, so sent round for a nominal roll of Saluties in the Division, to see if one could be attached to that Regiment.	
"	12.10.16		Went to Divisional Railhead at BEAURAINVILLE to inspect Remounts arriving, they were all apparently sound & free from disease.	
"	13.10.16		D.D.V.S. CAV CORPS visited the Division & inspected all the Mobile Vety Sections. We found that more drenching horns & mouth gags were required, there only being 1 of each in each Section. Inspected all animals of Signal Squadron 1st I.C.D. & found 5 horses in very poor condition; took notes of their numbers for further inspection at a later date. Horse float sent to MACHIEL to take a charger of Maj. MEYNELL 29th Lancers to No 22 Hospital ABBEVILLE. Received orders from D.D.V.S. Cav. Corps. to evacuate to No 22 or No 13 Hospitals.	MG
"	14.10.16		Inspected a Remount of Field Sqd. R.E. suspected of Mange, but was of opinion that itchiness was only due to a dirty skin. Visited Lucknow M.V.S. re appointing a Sergeant & Corporal to fill vacancies. Sent float to take a horse of Field Sqd RE to Lucknow MVS.	

WAR DIARY or INTELLIGENCE SUMMARY

Army Form C. 2118.

Place	Date	Hour	Summary of Events and Information	Remarks and references to Appendices
WADICOURT	16.10.16		Examined 5 cases of Debilitated Horses in the Signal Sqd 1st Div. 2 had Abnormalities of Teeth, 1 was old & worn out, 2 would improve with rest & careful feeding. Advised crushing of oats for whole squadron. Attended casting parade at SIALKOT CAV BDE with DDR. CAV CORPS. Informed DDVS/CAV CORPS that one Officers chest & 1 PM case was supplied for Mobile Vet Sections in this Division & not 2 of each as laid down in Equipment regulations. 18 Cases of Influenza in Divisional Ammunition Column RHA. most cases of a mild form, 2 severe. This unit had been in the open up to 2 weeks back, but now in billets. Ordered whole unit outside; had affected cases turned loose in a field; Incontacts & Convalescent all in separate groups. Systematic Taking of Temperatures daily. Reported to DDVS Cav Corps & AAQMG Division.	RPL
"	17.10.16		Visited Div Am. Col. RHA. 9 fresh cases Influenza admitted, all mildly affected except for high temperatures (103.6 to 105.6), congested conjunctiva & discharge from the eyes. All old cases doing well. CAPT. Bomfay AVC, OC MHon MVS evacuated to hospital "IRITIS".	
"	18.10.16		Advised Div HQ that the Ammunition Column should not move up to the front with the batteries until free from disease. DDVS CAV CORPS visited Ammunition Column with me, & we inspected every horse of the unit. 1 fresh case today. All others doing well, in spite of heavy rain during the night.	

WAR DIARY or INTELLIGENCE SUMMARY

Army Form C. 2118.

Place	Date	Hour	Summary of Events and Information	Remarks and references to Appendices
WADICOURT.	19.10.16		Visited "A" Bty RHA & saw a horse with fever. Simple but suspicious of Influenza, the battery was marching same day, so evacuated the animal to paddock where the Influenza cases of the Div Am Col were turned loose. Had all temperatures taken of horses in "A" Bty. all normal. Wired ADVS 1st Cav. Div. that A. Q & U Bty RHA were being detatched to join his division today, & for him to make veterinary arrangements. 5 fresh cases INFLUENZA in Div Amm Col. making 11 in all.	
"	" 20.10.16		1 case from SIALKOT. CAV. FD. AMBULANCE. Inspected Influenza cases in Amm Col. All doing well. No fresh cases. Rang up on telephone No 3 GEN L HOSPITAL, received information that Cap: Bonnavic would probably be evacuated to ENGLAND. Telephoned the DVS to this effect, & he said he would send me another Officer as soon as he received official information of this.	R.H.
"	" 21.10.16		AAQMG 1st ICD sent for me, & told me the CAV CORPS had received a report that the batteries detached from this Division to 1st CD had developed INFLUENZA. I informed him that they were clear of disease when they left. ODVS CAV CORPS & myself proceeded to CANAPLES & inspected all horses of A.Q.& U. Bty RHA & found them free from INFLUENZA. The report of disease had not emanated from the veterinary services. Reported Batteries free from disease to AAQMG 1st ICD.	

WAR DIARY or INTELLIGENCE SUMMARY

Army Form C. 2118.

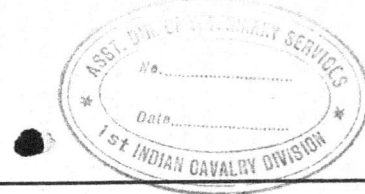

Place	Date	Hour	Summary of Events and Information	Remarks and references to Appendices
WADICOURT	22.10.16		Visited all 3 Mob Vety Sections & inspected the power clippers. Arranged to send 5 surplus AVC men from LUCKNOW MVS to No 2 Hospital HAVRE. 3 RHA Batteries rejoined the Division & also the VOs with them. Inspected the Influenza cases at the Ammunition Column, no fresh cases since 18th inst, all doing well, only 6 left with abnormal temperatures, but one case showing symptoms of Jaundice. Inspected a suspected Mange case at 19th Lancers (in contact with a case of Mange sent away a week ago) no lesions but extreme itchiness, advised evacuation.	
" "	23.10.16		Visited with DDVS. CAV CORPS the Influenza cases of Div Amm Col. RHA, there have been no fresh cases since 18th inst, & all temperatures of affected now normal. DDVS advised not moving the unit for another 10 days. Received wire from DVS. I.E.C through the Division that Lt BENNETT AVC (SR) had been ordered to join MHOW CAV BDE to take on the Mob. Vet. Section. Wired 13th Corps to arrange veterinary attendance for 155 animals of MACHINE GUNS attached to them from this division. Received wire from DDVS CAV CORPS asking if this division had left a horse behind at MOLLIENS VIDAME early in September during march to the front, sent messages to Staff Captains of Bdes & OC's Div Troops Units to find out.	R. 44.
" "	24.10.16		Arranged with AAQMG to give Div Amm Col. water troughs, instead of them watering in the river & perhaps contaminating other units. 13th CORPS wired for Map Reference of our MACHINE GUN SQUADRONS. also that the 31st Division would arrange for their Veterinary attendance.	

WAR DIARY or INTELLIGENCE SUMMARY

Army Form C. 2118.

Place	Date	Hour	Summary of Events and Information	Remarks and references to Appendices
WADICOURT	25.10.16		Visited 6th Cavalry & gave them labels from DADR. CAV. CORPS. to evacuate a horse cast by him. also went to MHOW M.V.S. & inspected 7 horses awaiting evacuation. gave orders to return one to its unit as it was not a case for L.V.C. hospital (eg. Wro. Punct. Foot). Arranged for the BVO MHOW. to visit MVS & send back to Hospital by road (ABBEVILLE).	
	26.10.16		also arranged for BVO to let me know date & time I could inspect 6th Dragoons. Telephoned DDVS CAV. CORPS ref veterinary attendance for FIELD SQD R.E. who marched to BOISMONT yesterday. Inspected Influenza cases of Div. Amm. Col. all doing well. Received memo from DADOS ref GRINDERS for sharpening blades of clipping machines, to which was attached a memo from C.O.O. saying that they were no use to us as men specially trained were required to use them. Forwarded correspondence to AAQMG & pointed out that an NCO in each MVS had been instructed in sharpening & renovating clipping blades with the Grinder, & had done so for all the units of the division last winter.	R.H.
	27.10.16		Inspected animals for evacuation at LUCKNOW M.V.S. Inspected horses & personnel of SIALKOT. M.V.S. Wired DDVS CORPS that no horse had been left behind by this division at MOLLIENS VIDAME. also that the 6th INNISKILLING DRAGOONS did not leave a horse at LOTTINGHEM. both these cases were horses left behind without proper FORMS being given the inhabitant.	
	28.10.16		Lt G.H. BENNETT AVC (SR) reported his arrival on 27" inst to command M.V.S MHOW CAV. BDE. Visited Jodhpur Lancers & saw 5 cases Influenza. Isolated Affected & In contact & took all precautions to prevent spread. Temperatures of Sqadrons to be taken	

WAR DIARY or INTELLIGENCE SUMMARY

(Erase heading not required.)

Army Form C. 2118.

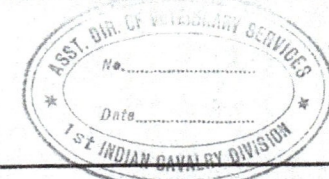

Place	Date	Hour	Summary of Events and Information	Remarks and references to Appendices
WADICOURT	28.10.16		Twice daily; & no work except walking exercise (A Sqd only affected) Reported ADVS Ambala. Inspected A & D Sqd 6th Dragoons. also 3 cases suspected Mange in 2nd Lancers. ordered 1 to be evacuated & 4 declared free.	
" "	29.10.16		No fresh cases of Influenza in Jodhpur Lancers. Inspected two cases of suspicious MANGE with LT STEVENS A.V.C. at AMBALA CAV FD AMB. ordered both to be evacuated, one case was very pronounced about neck & withers after clipping out. Received instructions that MAJOR J.A.B. McGONAN AVC would return to be ADVS of this Division on being relieved by Col. P.J. HARRIS AVC, & I would be DDVS Div Troops. This would make LT STEVENS/AVC surplus, he will proceed to 19th DIVISION to report to ADVS.	
" "	30.10.16.		No fresh cases INFLUENZA in Jodhpur Lancers.	
" "	31.10.16		Handed over charge to CAPT P.D. CAREY AVC from LUCKNOW MVS, back for me whilst on leave to England from 1st to 8th November.	

R.A. Goodricke
Major AVC
A.D.V.S. 1st Ind. Cav. Div.

CONFIDENTIAL.

WAR DIARY.

of

Assistant Director of Veterinary Services

4th Cavalry Division.

From 1=11=16. To 30=11=16.

(Volume V)

WAR DIARY ~~INTELLIGENCE SUMMARY~~

(Erase heading not required.)

Army Form C. 2118.

Instructions regarding War Diaries and Intelligence Summaries are contained in F. S. Regs., Part II. and the Staff Manual respectively. Title pages will be prepared in manuscript.

Place	Date	Hour	Summary of Events and Information	Remarks and references to Appendices
BERNAY	1-11-16		(1) Visited D.V.S. re-issuing proper orders for rendering recommendations of Veterinary Officers for mention in despatches or honours. (2) Arranged for MAJOR THURSTON. C.A.V.C. to be returned to the C.R.H.A. Bde 2nd, Indian Cavalry Division, and Capt. M.G. O'GOGARTY, C.A.V.C. to remain as Vety officer i/c Cavalry Corps Troops. (3) Major P.J. HARRIS, A.V.C. arrived to take over duties as D.D.V.S. Cavalry Corps from me.	
ST. VALERY	2-11-16		(1) Handed over office of D.D.V.S. Cavalry Corps to Major P.J. HARRIS, A.V.C. in the forenoon. (2) Took over duties of A.D.V.S. 1st Indian Cavalry Division. Major P.J. HARRIS A.V.C succeeded me as D.D.V.S. Cavalry Corps. He being senior in the A.V. Corps to myself. (3) 1st Indian Cavalry Division marched LEGISCOURT to a new billeting area, South of the River SOMME. Divl. Hd. Qrs. being at ST. VALERY. Lucknow Cav. Bde: Hd. Qrs = MOYENNEVILLE. " " M.V.S = HYMMEVILLE. Sialkote " " Hd. Qrs = PENDE. " " M.V.S = PENDE. Mhow " " Hd. Qrs = ESCARBOTIN, BELLOY. " " M.V.S = BELLOY.	

WAR DIARY or INTELLIGENCE SUMMARY.

(Erase heading not required.)

Army Form C. 2118.

Place	Date	Hour	Summary of Events and Information	Remarks and references to Appendices
ST. VALERY	3-11-16		(1) Attended to Divisional Headquarters sick.	
			(2) Lieut. B. PHILP. A.V.C. called at office re A-2000.	JABMcL
ST. VALERY	4-11-16		(1) Visited Siakote Mobile Vety. Sect. at PENDÉ.	
			(2) Received instructions from A.A. & Q.M.G to hand over my portable pack Forge to Colonel COBBE, A.A. & Q.M.G. 2nd Indian Cavalry Division, who had been instructed to take it first to the Cavalry Corps, and afterwards to the Quarter Master General with a view of procuring his sanction for the general issue of them to all Squadrons.	
			(3) Received NO. Q 4106 a/4-11-16, 1st I.C.D. re. 1st and 2nd Indian Cavalry Divisions and 3rd Cavalry Division, will be administered by Cavalry Corps, from 6th ins.	JABMcL
ST. VALERY	5-11-16		(1) Sent the Centrifugal Machine to O.C. M.V.S. Lucknow Cav. Bde.	
			(2) Capt H.B. WILLIAMS. A.V.C. called at office re Corpl C. de B. BARNETT, who has gone sick.	
			(3) A.D.V.S. 2nd Indian Cav. Divn called re the Dipping Bath which is going to be built at FRIVILLE.	
			(4) Capt C.M. BARTON. A.V.C. Mhow Cav. Bde applied for 4 days leave in PARIS. I refused it as he only arrived back from 8 days leave on the 11th Oct.	JABMcL

WAR DIARY ~~or INTELLIGENCE SUMMARY~~

Army Form C. 2118.

Instructions regarding War Diaries and Intelligence Summaries are contained in F. S. Regs., Part II. and the Staff Manual respectively. Title pages will be prepared in manuscript.

(Erase heading not required.)

Place	Date	Hour	Summary of Events and Information	Remarks and references to Appendices
ST. VALERY	6-11-16		(1) Arranged with A.A.&Q.M.G. to issue orders for units to return all horse shoes not tapped for Frost Cogs to D.A.D.O.S. who would issue tapped shoes in place of them.	
			(2) Arranged with A.A.&Q.M.G for men from Mohow Cav: Bde: to dig the hole for the Horse Dip either at FRIVILLE or BELLOY.	
			(3) Visited D.D.O.S. (Col. FORBES) G.H.Q. re: my Cavalry pack Forge, which the Q.M.G. has approved of, but wants the opinion of the D.V.S.	
			(4) Auxiliary Horse Transport Co: joined the Division & is billeted at FRESSENNEVILLE.	ADMS
" "	7-11-16		(1) Received the first official notice I have had of Capt A.B. BOWHAY, AVC being placed on the sick list and evacuated to England. I am passing the notification on to the A.D.M.S with the request that I may be informed immediately an officer of the A.V.C. is taken ill or excused duty owing to sickness.	
			(2) Visited M.V.S. Mohow Cav. Bde at BELLOY, inspected the men, horses and billets, everything was satisfactory. Since taking over the Section Lieut G.H. BENNET, A.V.C. has improved it considerably.	
			(3) Instructed Lieut: G.H. BENNET, to look round BELLOY for a good site	ADMS

WAR DIARY or INTELLIGENCE SUMMARY.

Army Form C. 2118.

Place	Date	Hour	Summary of Events and Information	Remarks and references to Appendices
ST. VALERY	7-11-16	Continued	site for the Horse Dipping Bath and report to me when he finds one.	
			(4) Visited 1st Field Squadron R.E. at BOISMONT and arranged by phone with O.C. No. 22 Vety. Hospital to send the motor ambulance out for two bad cases, one Wound Punctured Frog and the other Wound Punctured Stifle.	JHSMcC
"	8-11-16		(1) Visited Headquarters 29th Cavalry at CHEPY to see a suspicious case of mange in "A" Squadron (No. 113). I ordered its evacuation to the M.V.S.	
			(2) Visited Lucknow Cav. Bde Hd Qrs. at MOYENNEVILLE. Saw B.V.O. and instructed him to inspect all animals in the 29th Lancers for skin disease.	
			(3) Visited office of D.V.S. re: my Light Cavalry pack Forge, which is being sent to D.V.S. from G.H.Q. for report upon, but the D.V.S. was away on leave in England.	JHSMcC
"	9-11-16		(1) Capt. R.A. GOODERIDGE, A.V.C. returned from leave	
			(2) Temporary Major-General A.A. KENNEDY, C.M.G. from 7th Cavalry Bde assumed	JHSMcC

Instructions regarding War Diaries and Intelligence Summaries are contained in F. S. Regs., Part II. and the Staff Manual respectively. Title pages will be prepared in manuscript.

WAR DIARY

or

~~INTELLIGENCE SUMMARY.~~

(Erase heading not required.)

Army Form C. 2118.

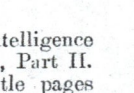

Place	Date	Hour	Summary of Events and Information	Remarks and references to Appendices
	Continued.			
ST: VALERY	9-11-16		assumed command of the 1st Indian Cavalry Division, vice Major General H.P. LEADER, C.B. appointed Inspector General of Cavalry in India.	
			(3) Arranged with A.A.&Q.M.G to issue an order that all horse shoes not tapped for frost cogs should be exchanged for shoes tapped.	
			(4) Visited and inspected the horses of the Auxiliary H.T.Co. at FRESSENNEVILLE and found their horses in fairly good condition. 91 were under cover and 141 are standing out in the open.	
			(5) The A.V.C. Sergt. (Sergt BYFORD) who is attached to this unit is not efficient enough in my opinion to be placed in Veterinary charge of this unit.	
			(5) Reported to A.A&Q.M.G the result of my inspection of Auxiliary H.T. Co.	JABMcG
" "	10-11-16		Office all day.	JABMcG
" "	11-11-16		Major J.A.B. McGOWAN, A.V.C. went on leave.	JABMcG
" "	12-11-16		Visited A.A&Q.M.G re: having another Shoeing-Smith on Establishment of Pioneer Battalion (76 horses). Correction already made bring it up to 1 Shoeing-Smith Corpl and 1 Shoeing-Smith.	JABMcG

T2134. Wt. W708—776. 500000. 4/15. Sir J. C. & S.

WAR DIARY ~~INTELLIGENCE SUMMARY~~
(Erase heading not required.)

Army Form C. 2118.

Place	Date	Hour	Summary of Events and Information	Remarks and references to Appendices
ST. VALERY	13-11-16		(1) Saw A.A. & Q.M.G. re getting authority from Cavalry Corps for Staff Pay and Pay of Temporary rank whilst acting as A.D.V.S. 1st Indian Cavalry Division. (2) Two cases of Influenza in Auxiliary H.T.Co. (3) Wrote A.A. & Q.M.G. re issue of Lime and Cresol for disinfecting horse billets. Calculated at 25% of horses occupying billets that could be disinfected.	JaBMcG
" "	14-11-16		(1) Visited Field Squadron R.E. and had sick lines changed. (2) Asked D.A.D.O.S. to supply another Power Clipper to Field Squadron, as their horses are carrying thick coats and sweating a lot at exercise. (3) Went No. 22 Veterinary Hospital to test A.A. & Q.M.G's horse.	JaBMcG
" "	15-11-16		(1) Visited Auxiliary H.T.Co with O.C. A.S.C. to classify draught horses, as regards getting an extra hay ration for extra heavy animals. Found about 30 horses rather above L.D. class. (2) Visited Lucknow and Ambala Cavalry Field Ambulances. (3) No more Influenza in Auxiliary H.T.Co.	JaBMcG

WAR DIARY or INTELLIGENCE SUMMARY

Army Form C. 2118.

Place	Date	Hour	Summary of Events and Information	Remarks and references to Appendices
ST. VALERY	16-11-16		(1) Visited Mhow M.V.S. re moving to FRIVILLE. (2) Wrote to A.A. & Q.M.G. re Divisional Ammunition Column, shoeing 3 chargers of Lucknow Casualty Clearing Station.	J.B. McQ
" "	17-11-16		Went BELLOY re horse left behind by 7th Canadian Cavalry Field Ambulance. Canadian Cavalry Bde. on April 9th 1916, and found it had been collected by "A" Canadian Mobile Veterinary Section, on November 13th 1916. ie 216 days. Y20 378	J.B. McQ
" "	18-11-16		Went No. 22 Veterinary Hospital saw Roaring Operation on 2 horses.	J.B. McQ
" "	19-11-16		(1) Asked A.A. & Q.M.G. re getting extra ration for 40 horses of Auxiliary H.T.Co. and recommended it to O.C. A.S.C. (2) Wired D.D.V.S. Cav. Corps re A & U Batteries moving "U" Battery R.H.A. joined 4th Army Artillery School "A" " " " 1st Division, 3rd Corps, 4th Army.	J.B. McQ

WAR DIARY

INTELLIGENCE SUMMARY.

(Erase heading not required.)

Army Form C. 2118.

Place	Date	Hour	Summary of Events and Information	Remarks and references to Appendices
ST. VALERY	20/11/16		Rang up Field Squadron R.E. re getting on with dipping baths; told they would begin in about 5 days time.	JABMcG
" "	21=11=16		(1) Returned from leave (MAJOR J.A.B. McGOWAN, A.V.C) Reported personally to D.D.V.S. Cavalry Corps, at BERNAY. (2) Capt P.D. CAREY, A.V.C. reported departure on leave to England.	JABMcG
" "	22-11-16		(1) Visited Auxiliary H.T. Co: at FRIVILLE, inspected a reported outbreak of Influenza amongst the horses of this unit and found 15 animals suffering from the disease. Ordered all animals in the unit to be picketed out in the open. (2) Reported the outbreak to the D.D.V.S. Cav Corps, by wire no: 56 and to G.O.C Division through the A.A & Q.M.G. (3) Pioneer Battalion of Lucknow Cav Bde joined 3rd Corps. 4th Army. Mhow Pioneer Battalion joined 1st Anzac Corps, 4th Army. Sialkote Cavalry Field ambulance joined 14th Corps. (4) Asked D.D.V.S. Cavalry Corps to arrange with D.D.V.S. 4th Army for Veterinary attendance on above units.	JABMcG

WAR DIARY

~~INTELLIGENCE SUMMARY~~

(Erase heading not required.)

Army Form C. 2118.

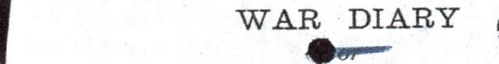

Place	Date	Hour	Summary of Events and Information	Remarks and references to Appendices
ST. VALERY	23.11.16		(1) Visited Divisional School at CAYEUX. Inspected Detachment of Auxiliary H.T. Co. horses there for Influenza and found 6 cases. Gave instructions for the whole Detachment to be picketed out.	
			(2) Warned O.C. 19 Lancers at CAYEUX of the outbreak and to take necessary preventive measures against the disease.	
			(3) Reported outbreak to Divisional Hd. Qrs. and D.D.V.S. Cavalry Corps.	
			(4) Four fresh cases of Influenza in Auxiliary H.T. Co. at FRIVILLE. One case of Influenza reported in Detachment of Auxiliary H.T. Co. at CHAUSSOY. Lucknow Cav. Bde.	
			(5) D.D.V.S. sanctioned Capt. H.B. WILLIAMS. Sialkote M.V.S. to proceed on 5 days leave to PARIS from Saturday 25-11-16.	HBMcg
" "	24.11.16		(1) D.D.V.S. Cavalry Corps, called at Office. I accompanied him to Auxiliary H.T. Co. at FRIVILLE and Detachment at CAYEUX. Inspected the Influenza cases and found them all progressing favourably.	
			(2) Visited the Detachment of Auxiliary H.T. Co. attached to Lucknow Cav. Bde Hd Qrs at CHAUSSOY. Inspected them for Influenza and saw the case reported yesterday. Ordered	HBMcg

WAR DIARY or INTELLIGENCE SUMMARY.

(Erase heading not required.)

Army Form C. 2118.

Place	Date	Hour	Summary of Events and Information	Remarks and references to Appendices
ST. VALERY	Continued 24-11-16		Ordered temperatures to be taken daily. (3) Visited the D.V.S. re my portable Cavalry Forge, but he had not received it yet from G.H.Q.	JaBmey
" "	25-11-16		(1) Capt. H.B. WILLIAMS, A.V.C. proceeded on 5 days leave to PARIS. (2) Lieut. B. PHILP, A.V.C. reported that all animals now billeted in Factory on VALINES-FRESSENNEVILLE Road had been inspected for Influenza and the temperatures were being taken daily. Title of 1st Indian Cav. Div. changed from the latter to 4th Cavalry Division from today	JaBmey
" "	26-11-16		(1) Visited 2nd Lancers at LANCHERE, inspected sick lines. (2) Mobile Veterinary Section, Lucknow Cav. Bde moved into billets at MOYENNEVILLE from HYMMEVILLE. (3) Lucknow Machine Gun Squadron rejoined the Bde and is billeted at HYMMEVILLE CAMPAGNE and QUESNOY. (4) Sialkote M.G. Squadron rejoined the Bde and is billeted at MONS and BOUBERT.	JaBmey

WAR DIARY or INTELLIGENCE SUMMARY

Army Form C. 2118.

Place	Date	Hour	Summary of Events and Information	Remarks and references to Appendices
ST. VALERY	27-11-16		(1) Redistributed veterinary charge of units in winter billets according to nearest veterinary officers.	
			(2) Recommended issue of a set of shoeing tools to all Farrier Sergeants, Corporal Shoeing-Smiths and Shoeing-Smiths, in British Cavalry Regiments, 18 per regiment and to all Farriers in Indian Cavalry Regiments, 16 per regiment. Asked the D.D.V.S. Cav: Corps to approve.	
"	28-11-16		(1) 4th Cavalry Division Reserve Park rejoined Division from 4th Army and is billeted at FRESSENNEVILLE	
			(2) Lieut. C.C. PARSONS, A.V.C. took over veterinary charge of the 2nd Lancers at LANCHERES, BRUTELLES and LALEU.	
			(3) Capt. C.M. BARTON, A.V.C. took over veterinary charge of the Auxiliary H.T. Co at FRIVILLE.	
			(4) Capt. R.A. GOODERIDGE, A.V.C. took over veterinary charge of 19th Lancers, Divisional School at CAYEUX.	

WAR DIARY

INTELLIGENCE SUMMARY

(Erase heading not required.)

Army Form C. 2118.

Place	Date	Hour	Summary of Events and Information	Remarks and references to Appendices
ST. VALERY	29-11-16		(1) Visited Ansciliary Horse Transport Co. at FRIVILLE. Inspected all the horses picketed out and ordered them back to billets again.	
			(2) Saw 21 cases suffering from Influenza running loose in a field. All their temperatures were normal and they were all progressing favourably.	
			(3) Visited 4th Cav. Divn Reserve Park at FRESSENNEVILLE. Inspected all the animals (199) which arrived yesterday. Several of them should be evacuated. I instructed Lieut. B. PHILP A.V.C. to arrange for their evacuation.	JaBMcG
" "	30-11-16		Office all day.	JaBMcG

30-11-16

Ja.P. McGowan
Major A.V.C.
A.D.V.S.
4th Cavalry Division

SERIAL NO. 322

Confidential War Diary

of

A.D.V.S., 4th Cavalry Division

FROM 1st December 1916 TO 31st December 1916

WAR DIARY / INTELLIGENCE SUMMARY

Army Form C. 2118.

Place	Date	Hour	Summary of Events and Information	Remarks and references to Appendices
ST. VALERY	1-12-16		(1) Office. (2) Capt. H.B. WILLIAMS, A.V.C. reported his return from leave in PARIS. (3) Memo no. 2051 dated 29-11-16, received from D.D.V.S. 4th Army, stating that he had made arrangements for veterinary attendance on the Lucknow and Mhow Pioneer Battalions of this Division, which are temporarily attached to the 4th Army.	HBMcC
"	2-12-16		(1) Office. (2) Accompanied D.D.V.S. Cavalry Corps on his inspection of Influenza cases in Auxiliary Horse Transport Co, and Horse Dip at FRIVILLE, Sialkote M.V.S. at PENDÉ and Mhow M.V.S. at BELLOY. (3) Inspected 2 suspicious mange cases in D Squadron 2nd Lancers at BRUTELLES and ordered them to be evacuated. One of them joined as a remount on the 26th Oct: 1916, and has been kept isolated and under observation ever since.	HBMcC
"	3-12-16		(1) Office. (2) Visited K.D. Gp: inspected suspicious mange case in "B" Squadron at MIANNAY. Ordered it to be evacuated. (3) Visited M.V.S. Lucknow Cav. Bde, inspected section and billets. Asked Brigade Major to give them better billets. (4) Visited no. 5 Veterinary Hospital re: latest improvements in Horse Dip.	HBMcC

WAR DIARY or INTELLIGENCE SUMMARY

Army Form C. 2118.

(Erase heading not required.)

Place	Date	Hour	Summary of Events and Information	Remarks and references to Appendices
ST. VALERY	4-12-16		(1) Office. (2) Visited Jodhpur Lancers. Inspected eleven horses being dressed with Sulphide of Calcium solution as suspicious mange cases.	JPMcY
,,	5-12-16		(1) Office all day.	JPMcY
,,	6-12-16		(1) Office. (2) Issued instructions to Lieut. B. PHILP, A.V.C.(T.C.) to report himself for duty with Lucknow Cav. Bde. as B.V.O. vice Capt. P.T. SAUNDERS, transferred to 5th Cav. Divn. (3) Issued instructions for Capt. P.T. SAUNDERS, A.V.C.(S.R.) to report himself for duty to A.D.V.S. 5th Cavalry Division. (4) Visited Ansciliary Horse Transport Co. and inspected the Convalescent Influenza cases with Capt. C.M. BARTON, V/O i/c and found them progressing favourably. (5) Called at Horse Dip, the R.E. were just commencing to cement the sides in. (6) Visited K.D.Gs: inspected 2 suspicious cases of mange. Ordered Capt. SAUNDERS, to take scrapings and report. (7) Visited No. 5 Veterinary Hospital and saw the Horse Dip when it was empty and got all particulars as to the working of it from Major WADLEY, A.V.C. (8) Visited Cavalry Corps Headquarters; D.D.V.S. Office, for whom I am officiating whilst he is on leave to England.	JPMcY

WAR DIARY / INTELLIGENCE SUMMARY

Army Form C. 2118.

Place	Date	Hour	Summary of Events and Information	Remarks and references to Appendices
ST. VALERY	7.12.16	(1)	Major J.A.B. McGOWAN, A.V.C. proceeded to Cavalry Corps Hd Qrs. to take up the duties of D.D.V.S. Cavalry Corps, whilst Colonel P.J. HARRIS, A.V.C. is away on leave to the 16th December.	JaBMcG
"	8-12-16	(1)	O.C. M.V.S. Mhow Cav. Bde reported no accommodation in FRIVILLE for M.V.S. Saw A.A. & Q.M.G about it and he said he would write O.C. A.S.C. to tell him to ask O.C. Ausciliary H.T. Co to make room.	JaBMcG
"	9.12.16	(1)	Capt. P.T. SAUNDERS, A.V.C. transferred to 5th Cavalry Division.	JaBMcG
		(2)	Lieut B. PHILP, A.V.C transferred from Divisional Amm. Column R.H.A to Lucknow Cav. Bde.	
"	10.12.16	(1)	Office.	JaBMcG
"	11.12.16	(1)	Visited Mobile Vety. Section Mhow Cav. Bde, saw mob. vet Sect animals and 1 sick from Field Squadron R.E.	JaBMcG
"	12.12.16	(1)	Examined tin plates in the feet of 6 horses of Field Squadron R.E. Had lasted well having been in 3½ weeks.	JaBMcG

WAR DIARY

Army Form C. 2118.

(Erase heading not required.)

Place	Date	Hour	Summary of Events and Information	Remarks and references to Appendices
ST: VALERY	13-12-16		(1) Went K.D.Gs, saw Glanders and mange cases. Lieut B. PHILP A.V.C. re-tested Glanders case in neck.	A&BMcG
"	14-12-16		Inspected Divisional Headquarters' animals owing to a case of mange in one of the mules.	A&BMcG
"	15-12-16		(1) Went K.D.Gs and met D.D.V.S. re Post mortem examination on Glanders case. No lesions except ulcers in nostrils. Decided to Mallein whole of "A" Squadron.	A&BMcG
"	16-12-16		(1) Office.	A&BMcG
"	17-12-16		(1) Saw A.A.+Q.M.G. re shoeing of a squadron of each regiment with protector for picked-up-Nail.	A&BMcG
"	18-12-16		(1) Assumed the duties of A.D.V.S. 4th Cavalry Division from officiating D.D.V.S. Cav Corps.	A&BMcG
"	19-12-16		(1) Office. (2) Visited School of Farriery at ABBEVILLE and obtained some dried specimens of hoofs for lecturing on at the Divisional School. (3) Interviewed D.V.S. re the G.S. limber wagons in Mob. Vet. Sections being replaced by G.S. wagons. I reported that G.S. limber wagons were very necessary for Cavalry M.V. Sections.	A&BMcG

WAR DIARY

INTELLIGENCE SUMMARY
(Erase heading not required.)

Army Form C. 2118.

Place	Date	Hour	Summary of Events and Information	Remarks and references to Appendices
ST. VALERY	20-12-16		(1) Office all day.	JaBMcG
"	21-12-16		(1) Office. (2) Visited Sialkote Cavalry Bde Headquarters and Mobile Veterinary Section at PENDE. Inspected Section horses, mules and Transport. (3) Arranged with O.C. Divisional School at CAYEUX, to give Demonstration on the points of the horse and shoeing from 12 noon to 1 P.M. and 2.30 to 3.30 P.M. on Tuesday the 26th December.	JaBMcG
"	22-12-16		(1) Office all day.	JaBMcG
"	23-12-16		(1) Office. (2) Visited and inspected 9 suspicious mange cases in 29th Lancers at CHEPY, gave instructions to have them re-clipped, well groomed for 4 days and scrapings taken and examined, when I will see them again. (3) Visited Lucknow M.V.S. inspected men, horses, & billets. (4) Visited Mhow M.V.S. inspected men, horses & billets.	JaBMcG
"	24-12-16		(1) Office. (2) Visited 2nd Lancers at LANCHERES. Inspected 9 suspicious cases of mange. Instructed them to be clipped out, thoroughly groomed and scrapings taken.	JaBMcG

WAR DIARY ~~INTELLIGENCE SUMMARY~~

(Erase heading not required.)

Army Form C. 2118.

Place	Date	Hour	Summary of Events and Information	Remarks and references to Appendices
ST. VALERY	25/12/16		(1) Xmas Day.	
"	26.12.16		(1) Office. (2) Lectured at Divisional School CAYEUX on points of Horse and seats of common 12 P.M. to 1 P.M. (3) Lectured at Divisional School CAYEUX on shoeing 2.30 P.M. to 3.30 P.M.	
"	27.12.16		(1) Office. (2) No. S.E.11739 Unpaid Acting Sergt. J.A. KETCHELL, A.V.C. joined Auxiliary H.T. Co on 26.12.16 from No. 2 Veterinary Hospital HAVRE. (3) Capt H.B. WILLIAMS. A.V.C. reported his arrival from leave in England. (4) Visited 29th Lancers at CHEPY. Inspected all animals in "A" Squadron and discovered 19 suspicious mange cases. Instructed Lieut. B. PHILP. to take scrapings and report results. Inspected the 9 cases of Sarcoptic mange in A Squadron previously seen and corroborated by microscopical examination of scrapings. (5) Reported to G.O.C. Division, Lucknow Cav. Bde & D.D.V.S. Cavalry Corps that 9 cases of Sarcoptic mange had been discovered in 'A' Squadron 29th Lancers. (6) Capt R.A. GOODERIDGE. A.V.C. proceeded on 5 days leave to PARIS.	

WAR DIARY or INTELLIGENCE SUMMARY

(Erase heading not required.)

Army Form C. 2118.

Place	Date	Hour	Summary of Events and Information	Remarks and references to Appendices
ST. VALERY	28-12-16		(1) Office. (2) D.D.V.S. Cav. Corps, called at office for me. We inspected Lucknow M.V.S at CHAUSSOY and found everything satisfactory. (3) Inspected the suspicious mange cases in 29th Lancers at CHEPY. (4) Inspected the 2 Influenza cases in Auxiliary Horse Transport Co at FRIVILLE	
"	29-12-16		(1) Office. (2) Inspected 29 Lancers horses at CHEPY and ACHEUX for mange and found a number of suspicious cases. 16 in "A" Squadron, 4 in "B" Squadron, 2 in C Squadron and 2 in D Squadron (3) Inspected all horses & mules in Divisional Headquarters.	JPMcG JPMcG
"	30-12-16		(1) Office.	JPMcG
"	31-12-16		(1) Office (2) Inspected horses of Signal Squadron Divisional Headquarters and found them in fair condition and the shoeing good. (3) Visited Field Squadron R.E at BOISMONT. Inspected the sick animals and 5 cases of Ringworm. Advised O.C. to continue dressing them. (4) Consulted G.O.C. on measures to prevent Picked-Up-Nail, by placing tin plates or pieces hoop iron between the shoe and sole.	

31=12=16

J.P. McGowan
Major A.V.C
A.D.V.S
4th Cav. Divn

www.ingramcontent.com/pod-product-compliance
Lightning Source LLC
Chambersburg PA
CBHW081238170426
43191CB00034B/1969